"In a classic fashion, Florence Littaue
ence's lifelong study of the Personalities with timely, contemporary
applications for small-business owners, entrepreneurs, and ministry
leaders. The chapter 'Personalities and Multilevel Marketing' gives
valuable insight for individuals and couples involved in any multilevel
direct-sales organization. If you want to know how to successfully
work with anyone, this book is a must-read!"

> **John H. Thurman Jr.**, MDiv, MA, licensed clinical professional
> counselor; Five Diamond Designer, Premier Designs Jewelry

"My friend Florence Littauer has taught me more about the Personalities than any other person. Run, don't walk, to buy this book. You
will be glad you did!"

> **John C. Maxwell**, author and speaker

"Positive relationships with co-workers are an integral part of how
any organization can continue to grow and evolve in changing times.
Littauer takes a thought-provoking look at various Personalities and
how best to utilize them to achieve the greatest success."

> **Dr. Nido Qubein**, president, High Point University;
> chairman, Great Harvest Bread Company

"In my career I've used any number of the 'latest and greatest' management techniques to improve my bottom-line. But it always comes down
to really knowing and understanding Personalities, whether it's my
boss, peers, or employees. I highly recommend that everyone not just
read *Personality Plus at Work* but give it real thought and consciously
identify the Personalities of those around you in the workplace. It will
prove invaluable!"

> **Ed Bennett**, PE, LEED AP, executive director for physical plant and
> deputy for facilities management, Virginia Commonwealth University

"I've consulted with Rose for years about personnel problems in my
mortgage, title, and escrow companies. Thanks to understanding the
Personalities—and particularly how to successfully blend them—I
now have the perfect team. Their strengths compliment each other and
offset their weaknesses. Using what we've learned from the Personalities, we've doubled our gross annual income!"

> **Malia Monroe**, owner, Four Seasons Mortgage Company

"Florence Littauer and Rose Sweet take you by the hand and lead you
to that 'aha' moment for the workplace."

> **Ron Chapman**, National Association of Broadcasters "Hall of Fame"

Other Personality Plus Books Available

Personality Plus
Personality Plus for Couples
Personality Plus for Parents

Personality
PLUS
at WORK

How to Work
Successfully with Anyone

FLORENCE LITTAUER
ROSE SWEET

Revell

a division of Baker Publishing Group
Grand Rapids, Michigan

© 2011 by Florence Littauer and Rose Sweet

Published by Revell
a division of Baker Publishing Group
P.O. Box 6287, Grand Rapids, MI 49516-6287
www.revellbooks.com

Printed in the United States of America

Library of Congress Cataloging-in-Publication Data
Littauer, Florence, 1928–
    Personality plus at work : how to work successfully with anyone / Florence Littauer, Rose Sweet.
        p.   cm.
    Includes bibliographical references (p.   ).
    ISBN 978-0-8007-3054-3 (pbk.)
    1. Personality. 2. Interpersonal relations. 3. Success in business. 4. Success in business—Religious aspects—Christianity. I. Sweet, Rose, 1951– II. Title.
    BF698.L543 2011
    158.7—dc22   2010038937

The characters and events in this book are fictitious. Any similarities to real persons, living or dead, are coincidental and not intended by the authors.

11 12 13 14 15 16 17   7 6 5 4 3 2 1

In keeping with biblical principles of creation stewardship, Baker Publishing Group advocates the responsible use of our natural resources. As a member of the Green Press Initiative, our company uses recycled paper when possible. The text paper of this book is comprised of 30% post-consumer waste.

Contents

Contents

The Four Personalities according to Hippocrates (ca. 400 BC)

The Popular Personality: Sanguine
Fun, outgoing, optimistic . . . but disorganized and too chatty

The Powerful Personality: Choleric
Goal-oriented, born leader, confident . . . but bossy and insensitive

The Perfect Personality: Melancholy
Deep, thoughtful, organized . . . but negative and often depressed

The Peaceful Personality: Phlegmatic
Pleasant, easygoing, adaptable . . . but indecisive and unmotivated

Cast of Characters

Our Students	Their Personalities	Their Story
Carmen Gonzalez	MELANCHOLY Phlegmatic	Timid schoolteacher who wants to know how to better understand her students.
Dr. Charles Everett Hastings III	MELANCHOLY Phlegmatic	Wealthy surgeon who has a dry wit and seems rather condescending.
Holly Homes	SANGUINE Phlegmatic	Flashy real estate agent who likes to laugh and be the center of attention.
Howard Jones	SANGUINE Choleric	Talkative restaurateur who has a jelly belly.
Darlene Guttenberg	CHOLERIC Melancholy	Domineering executive who works with husband Hans in multilevel marketing (MLM).
Fran Taylor	CHOLERIC Sanguine	Outgoing women's clothing executive who never misses an opportunity to sell.
Hans Guttenberg	PHLEGMATIC Melancholy	Wimpy husband of Darlene who works with her in MLM.
Pastor Paul Page	PHLEGMATIC Melancholy	Quiet pastor whose sermons put his congregation to sleep.

Say Hello to the Cast of Characters

It was a rainy afternoon in April when Rose and I (Florence) walked into the Loma Linda University library to begin a series of lectures we called "Personality Plus at Work." The dean, Dr. Hemingway, had scheduled these classes based on a perceived need of people who would often complain to him. They would ask, "How can I understand all these mixed-up people I have to deal with in my workplace?" or, "When I have the answers, why won't people just do it my way?"

Dr. Hemingway wasn't sure how to handle these questions, until one evening he met me at a dinner party and began to explain how frustrated he was.

"People talk to me as if I could prescribe a magical pill they could take each morning and suddenly be wise. We all know there's no such thing!" He slammed down his fork in disgust.

I smiled. "Well, Dr. Hemingway, there actually *is* a mystery cure for personality problems, and I'd love to explain it to you. It comes from your own profession—from a Greek physician in 400 BC—and it still works today."

"Really?" he asked.

"You remember Hippocrates? He asked the same questions as you: 'Is there some way I might understand my patients?' and 'Why don't they all react the same way to the same instructions?'"

Our discussion got so exciting as we shared back and forth, problem and solution, that soon others around us were listening and wanting to hear more. From that conversation came the idea for a sixteen-week course on "Personality Plus at Work" . . . and here we were, Rose and I, walking into a classroom where eight selected people were waiting for us. Four men and four women—from different corners of the business world—who needed help with "all those people who are nothing like me."

Rose and I had been teaching the four personalities as a fun way to get along with difficult people, but we had never tried it with such a handpicked group. Dr. Hemingway had invited friends and professionals alike to prepare for the course by reading my book *Personality Plus* and by taking the Personality Profile included in the back of this book. When we arrived for our first session, we knew the personalities of our eight students and we were ready for them.

Let's Meet the Group

I started by explaining to the students that Rose and I were both blends of the Choleric-Sanguine personalities and that as we went through the course they would understand more about what that meant. Rose added, "That means we both like to be in charge, but don't worry—we'll make it fun!"

"Yes," I agreed. "We both like to be in charge." I looked right at Rose.

"In charge! Right! Yes, Florence is teaching today. You'll have to wait for me to take over next time!" Rose smiled at the group and then took a seat in the back of the room. As Sanguines, we have learned how to work with one another in our teaching assignments. We enjoy being playful but are always respectful with each other.

10

After we had introduced ourselves, I asked each student to give their name and their reason for being here, in order of how they were sitting. I started with a relaxed young woman with big brown eyes and dark curly hair.

"I'm **Carmen Gonzalez**. I'm a teacher at the local high school, and I'm hoping to understand my pupils better. They're all so different, and some don't even want to be in school. I read your book, Florence—*Personality Plus*—and I think I'm *Melancholy* because I love to study and I get easily depressed with the antics of these teenagers!"

Next was a middle-aged lady, somewhat chubby, with bright blue eyes and an eagerness to tell us who she was. "I'm **Darlene Guttenberg**, and I'm here to learn more about my business associates. I'm in network marketing and I work, work, work all the time. My mind never seems to shut down!" I knew right away she was *Choleric*.

Next at the table was a quiet, unresponsive man who hadn't smiled yet. "I wouldn't have come here by myself, but my wife, Darlene," he nodded his head toward the woman next to him, "dragged me here. That's what she does with me, but I don't mind. My name is Hans. **Hans Guttenberg**." I looked over at Rose and we both exchanged a silent word: *Phlegmatic*.

The group seemed confused. Should they feel sorry for Hans being dragged around or glad that he had Darlene to pep him up?

Next was an eager man who looked as if he'd really enjoyed eating his whole life. Like Santa Claus, when he laughed his belly shook like jelly. "I'm **Howard Jones**. Since I'm in the restaurant business some people think I'm Howard Johnson! My problem is how to keep the help. It seems as soon as I get them trained, they leave. I'm sick of all these flaky people and I hope I can get a few who'll stay. I read your book, too, Florence, and I'm pretty sure I'm *Choleric*. I'd like being in charge more if any of them would actually listen."

"You think *you've* got problems!" yelled out the blonde next to Howard. She wore a tight T-shirt that read **HOLLY HOMES**. "You

11

should be in real estate. I don't know who is more difficult—the crazy salespeople in my office or the weird looky-loos who come in. You could mix them all up in one bowl and you couldn't make a decent pancake. That's what my mother—God rest her soul—used to say. You probably noticed that I'm Holly. My last name is not really 'Homes,' but it works better. I love to have fun at work, but lately there hasn't been much of it. This market *sucks*!"

Sanguine! Rose and I exchanged silent smiles.

After Holly's last comment, the dignified, tall, thin man next to Holly moved his chair a little farther away from her. "I'm **Pastor Paul Page**, and I like peace and quiet. I'm here because my people think I'm not exciting enough. One man even told me, 'When you start preaching, I go right to sleep.' He's one of the elders, too, so that's not good. I hope I can improve my personality, although I'm happy with it myself."

"You're *Phlegmatic*!" said Howard. "Right, Florence?" I nodded and noticed the pastor looked as if he needed to say something else. "I've never been married because I guess I have trouble making important decisions," he added, and laughed softly.

Holly moved her chair a little closer to him and smiled broadly.

On the other side of the single, spiritual pastor sat an obviously worldly and color-coordinated young woman with perfect makeup and extra eyelashes. "I'm **Fran Taylor**, and I'm into women's clothes."

"You sure are, honey!" Howard tossed in.

"Thank you, sir. What I mean is I supervise a chain of retail stores and work in the main office when I'm not traveling. This takes a lot of hands-on work, and I really have two full-time jobs—although they don't see it that way. I don't get two salaries!" She laughed at this, then started in again.

"I *love* clothes. I *love* people. I *love* to talk, and I *love* to be in charge. There are so many things I love that I might even be a split personality! Well, we have a whole new line of jewelry, and these new brochures I brought show the elegant finish on the gold and the brilliant colored stones. They almost look real, don't they? But you'll *love* the price! As it says here in the front, 'So much for so little'! I brought order forms for everyone and—yes—I take credit cards."

As Fran passed out her promotional material I called on our last person, a handsome, intelligent-looking—and obviously wealthy— gentleman.

"I'm **Dr. Charles Everett Hastings III.** The other two aren't with me—they're dead." He smiled at his attempted humor, even though no one else did.

"But they were both doctors, and I had no choice. To fulfill the family legacy I had to become 'the third.' So I attended Phillips Andover Academy, Harvard, and I have an MD from Princeton." He paused so we could all let the degrees sink in.

"Why am I here when I'm already overeducated? Because Dr. Hemingway told me to come, to 'get away from all those intellectual snobs and spend some time with normal people who don't care about my IQ.' Just go and be a nice person. I actually learned about Hippocrates in med school, but I never used it. Thought it was too simple for me. So here I am—out with ordinary people—but I must admit that listening to you all, you do seem to be a pleasant group."

By the time the good doctor finished, no one knew what to think. Should they be insulted? Or should they feel sorry that he was so out of touch?

I thanked everyone for introducing themselves and then pulled out an old magazine cover to begin our course, which starts in our next chapter.

As you read along with us, picture that you, too, have been specially handpicked and are with us in your seat, ready to go! Soon these people's problems will relate to yours, and our solutions will brighten your day. We're glad you're part of our "pleasant group"!

PART 1

OVERVIEW
OF THE
PERSONALITIES

1

Where Do the Personalities Come From?

As I (Florence) held up a copy of *Time* magazine from July 3, 2000, I opened the class by reading them the story of how two teams of geneticists had completed the discovery of every inherited trait in the human body. "After more than a decade of dreaming, planning, and heroic number crunching," I read from the article, "both groups have deciphered essentially all the 3.1 billion biochemical 'letters' of human DNA, the coded instructions for building and operating a fully functional human."[1]

I explained that among those identified traits, such as eye color, hair texture, body shape, and size of nose, was also personality. We come into this world with our own little nature, our own pattern of behavior, and our own natural reactions to people. We may be introverts or extroverts—or a combination of both—just as we may be tall or short or somewhere in between.

"If you have gray eyes and you want them to be blue," I said, "you can buy contact lenses in several colors, but when you take out the lenses your eyes are still gray. If you want your dark hair to be blonde, you can bleach it. But when the new growth comes out, it's your natural color—brown."

"That's right!" It was Holly Homes, the Sanguine real estate agent. "I always wanted to be a blonde!" She laughed at herself, even though very few others in the group did.

We come into this world with our own little nature, our own pattern of behavior, and our own natural reactions to people.

I continued. "The same is true of your inherited personality. Outside influences like social environment, family dynamics, age, maturity level, or even birth order may have shaped it—making your 'brown' personality appear 'blonde'—but at the root of it all is always your true temperament.

"Parents who know this handle their children according to their individual birth personality. If they treat all their children the same, some will flourish, some will rebel, and some will give up trying to please Mother. We'd be aghast at the thought of trying to dye our two-year-old's hair, but we might think nothing of trying to change her personality to make her be like her older sister.

"As I deal with people's adult personality problems—many of which show up at work—I often find that their parents wanted them to be a different type than what they are, often asking their children, What is the matter with you? Why are you so difficult? or even Why can't you be like your brother?"

Dr. Hastings sighed audibly when I said this, and added, "Just what *my mother* told me."

Rose and I again exchanged glances, knowing that over the next few weeks we were sure to discover some of the personal stories of this group. But right now we had a lot of material to cover, so I went on.

"Children who grow up somehow thinking they are a disappointment to their parents may spend their life looking for someone who will like them as they are. And if they don't find a place where their personality is appreciated, they will experience problems."

When we study the personalities, we'll understand why we are not all alike. We will see how each of us can make a unique contribution to the world—and learn to appreciate the contributions of others.

Source of the Funny Names

"Let's take a short break and when we come back, let's look at a little history. Medical history," I said. At this, Dr. Charles Everett Hastings III seemed to perk up a little.

When everyone returned, I shared about Hippocrates, a Greek philosopher and physician who lived about 400 BC and experienced difficulty with his patients. Some of them did what he recommended, and some did not. He wondered why. What made some patients compliant while others were so much more difficult? His questions led him to begin the first known study of personalities. He examined the body fluids in his patients and came up with four categories, now known as the classic "temperaments."

After I explained this, I moved to the chart we had on the wall behind the lectern and said, "Enough with history; now for a quick vocabulary lesson." I shared the basic definitions of the four personalities:

Sanguine (from red, hot blood) is a person who is lively, fun-loving, optimistic, popular, and an enthralling storyteller. This person can also be self-focused and forgetful.

Choleric (from yellow bile) is a person who loves to be in charge and wants control. This person may also be self-centered, impatient with others, bossy, and quick to anger.

Melancholy (from black bile) is a person who sees the details, is introspective, and desires perfection. This person tends to be

19

easily depressed, pessimistic, and often doesn't enjoy social gatherings that involve making conversation with people he or she doesn't know or may not like.

Phlegmatic (from phlegm) is a low-key, easygoing, and agreeable person who likes to relax and may appear to others to be lazy. This person is a steady worker and is best at giving strong support to others but isn't naturally goal-oriented or extremely driven to achieve.

According to the *Encyclopedia Britannica*, in psychology, "temperament" is the aspect of personality concerned with emotional dispositions and reactions and their *speed* and *intensity*.

Speed

Cholerics and Sanguines move *quickly*.

Melancholies and Phlegmatics move more *deliberately*.

Intensity

Cholerics and Melancholies are *intense* and *deep*.

Phlegmatics and Sanguines are *easygoing* and *light*.

"While Hippocrates's theory about body fluids as the origin of temperament isn't taught as much today," I told our class, "his observations about human behavior were right on and have proved accurate for more than two thousand years."

I asked Rose to come up and share another interesting fact.

"I first learned the temperaments in my Catholic high school," she said. "The teachings on temperaments were preserved through the centuries by monks who used them as an aid in spiritual development to 'know thyself' and to understand how to more effectively meet others' needs. This encouraged them to focus on the whole person—emotions, passions, natural tendencies, reactions, virtues, and spiritual gifts. Thomas Aquinas, one of the most brilliant philosophers in Western civilization, wrote about temperament and its relation to virtue in his famous *Summa Theologica*, a commentary still used today by students in law, ethics, theology, philosophy, and psychology. He wrote: 'Three things are necessary for the salvation of man: to know what he ought to believe, to know what he ought to desire, and to know what he ought to do.'"[2]

"Thank you, Rose," I said, and turned to the class. "When you understand the personalities, you'll be following Thomas Aquinas's sage advice to believe the best of others, to know what they desire, and to know what you ought to do to appreciate and get along with them—especially in the workplace."

Our Fathers' Businesses

After this quick overview—and before we started more teaching—I wanted everyone to know why Rose and I had pursued the study of the personalities and how we ended up teaching this class and writing this book.

"Both Rose and I grew up in our fathers' businesses," I said. "Her father ran a real estate development and appraisal company out of their home, and I grew up living and working in my father's small variety store."

The conversations my family had in the kitchen could be heard by the customers in the store. If we were talking about someone, and that person walked into the store, my father would warn us by suddenly singing loudly, "Holy, holy, holy . . ." If I'm in a church today, and they sing this hymn, I immediately shut my mouth. This was how my training on getting along with everybody began.

My two brothers and I grew up to be speakers: Jim was an Air Force chaplain and colonel with many honors, and Ron is the most popular radio personality in the Dallas, Texas, area. We all look back to our time in the store as the foundation for our success in effective communication.

Rose is the oldest of eight children and a fun-loving Sanguine in a serious Melancholy family. She had to be a junior mother to all the little ones, and that was just fine for Rose, whose personality was a combination of happy-go-lucky Sanguine and take-charge Choleric. Life was most fun when she could come up with games or contests for everyone to play. During these activities, Rose would boss everyone around, and if anyone complained, she'd remind them how much fun they were having. Her dad was a boss, too, and sometimes she'd sneak into his home office and listen to him transact business on the phone. When he would get a break, Rose would try to share cute little stories, but he would eventually bark, "Get to the point, Rosie; get to the point!" He was a Choleric-Melancholy trying to run a big business and support a large family and, being impatient, sometimes was no fun.

Rose also loved being in school, but most of the Melancholy nuns didn't find her classroom antics very funny. In her high school humanities class, her teacher, Sister Maria, shared about Hippocrates and the four basic personalities. Rosie loved finding out about herself and learning that wanting to have fun was not bad. However, when the teacher got to the Sanguine weaknesses, Rosie recognized many of the faults that her family had constantly pointed out to her. She felt ashamed, as if the whole classroom knew the Sanguine weaknesses were all about her!

We've found that most people love their strengths but don't like to look at their weaknesses. Rose didn't want anyone to notice *she* had any weaknesses. She didn't seem to fit anywhere, and so she decided she would change herself into the Melancholy that the teacher said was more saintly and that her parents said was more perfect. She sat quietly beside her father, told her stories quickly and to the point, and learned his business. After attending the University of San Francisco, Rose returned to her father's office and worked hard to learn how to evaluate and analyze commercial real estate properties. To compete in a male-dominated industry, she had to play Melancholy and push down her Sanguine bubbles. This was no fun either! But her charm was appealing to the clients and she was soon running the business. When Rose brought her staff to hear me speak on the personalities, she was confused. Was she a serious Melancholy real estate appraiser or was she a Sanguine hiding her light under a business bushel?

As I observed Rose in that audience, I saw a striking beauty with a Sanguine smile and excitement. When I got to the Sanguine strengths, her employees pointed at her and said, "That's you!" Afterward, Rose and I talked about her life and concluded she was a repressed Sanguine living as a Melancholy businesswoman. "That was the first time I'd ever felt free," she told me. It was as if we'd let the real Rose stand up and accept herself as God meant her to be.

"Now Rose travels as a speaker on relationships in the workplace," I told our class, "combining her personal experience with her engaging personality and humor." The group was listening intently, but I noticed they were looking over at Rose, who sat smiling—and a little tearful—as I told her story. Rose added, "Yes, I will be forever thankful that Florence tells my story *even better* than I could tell it myself!" We all laughed, breaking the mood, and I continued.

"We learned training and self-discipline in our fathers' businesses that kept us from problems in working with all kinds of people, but it wasn't until we both discovered the four personalities that we understood why those other people weren't like us."

I've been studying, speaking, and writing about "Personality Plus" for forty years, and Rose—after hearing me teach on the subject—began to apply the principles in her father's business and all her relationships as well. Because of her twenty years of study, writing five books, and love for others, she has become an expert on human relationships and serves with me as staff for our advanced speaker training, called "Upper Class." We're both Sanguines with a cup of Choleric stirred in; we want to have fun and have it done our way. We get along best with people who understand this.

"We have both been asked over the years to write a book on 'Personality Plus' in the workplace, so finally we have done it." I smiled at our class. "If you have enjoyed my book *Personality Plus*, you will love this new application; and if you have not read the first book, please read that also. We can guarantee that you will relate better with the difficult people in your life and even enjoy doing it."

I was happy to see our audience listening intently at this new information. But was it useful information? Or just another bit of pop psychology? I could see the question in their eyes.

Useless Information or Essential Data?

To answer this question, I gave a personal example from my own life, as I usually do.

"One day I was talking with my bright, twenty-two-year-old grandson, Bryan. He works with his father in their store buying and selling gold, and he mentioned how some of the customers seemed desperate to cash in their jewelry—even their wedding rings—to get money. We discussed the whole national financial crunch and I quoted Shakespeare: 'Neither a borrower nor a lender be.' In other words, be cautious about both borrowing and lending. He liked the quote and asked me, 'Who said that?'

"Shakespeare," I answered. "Didn't you study Shakespeare in school?"

"No, they don't teach that stuff anymore. There's no reason to clutter up your brain with information you'll never use."

Well, I had never thought of learning that way. Did I waste my college time with things I would never use? After my three years of Latin, had anyone ever asked me to conjugate a verb or even care about *amo, amas, amat*? All that math and solid geometry! No one ever asked me how many ounces are in a quart or how to

24

measure an acre. *Maybe Bryan's right,* I thought, *and my mind is cluttered up with unused information.*

Then he summed it up for me, pointing to his ever-present Black-Berry, as he explained, "You don't need to know anything anymore, as long as you know where to find it." Carried to its extreme, in twenty years no one will know anything. "But they'll have baskets full of BlackBerries," I joked.

Darlene Guttenberg, the sharp and obviously successful marketing executive, interrupted quickly by raising her hand and showing the group her BlackBerry. "Can't live without it," she said. A few others nodded in agreement.

Had I ever realized that my heavy brain might be full of untapped information? Can I clean up my cache with a delete button? As I thought this over, I realized that many things I've learned in life are not facts from a college course or hunted up on a BlackBerry but are valuable information nonetheless: knowing how to get along with people, being sensitive to others' pain, or understanding why a customer doesn't respond. Many of our relationship skills are a combination of these understandings, learned in a lifetime of experiences. My knowledge is like a cushion—it makes me comfortable; I can lean back on it and relax.

That's the reason we know that the simple tool of understanding the personalities is not useless information. It will help you get along with difficult people, something you can't learn by hitting "search" on the computer. When a client comes in late, flustered, and full of excuses about the traffic, she doesn't want a lecture on watches. She wants to tell you her traumatic story and have you listen and respond accordingly. When my husband, Fred, and I had an office together, we had a name for this need: the Poor Baby Syndrome. When a Sanguine employee came in late and had tragic—yet hilarious—excuses, we'd give her hugs, pat her gently, and say, "Poor baby, poor baby." This would feed her emotional need, and then she could get to work.

The exact opposite—the Melancholy—would react differently. In the first place, the organized Melancholy plans carefully and ahead of time. He allows for possible accidents, tornadoes, and landslides and expects something bad will happen. Even if the problem for being late were unavoidable, he would arrive repentant and offer to work late to make up for the time he lost.

The Choleric loves work, seldom makes mistakes, and is never to blame for any adverse circumstance. If she does make a mistake, she will—without hesitation—prove that it was someone else's fault. She may well get in early and work late, but the other employees don't appreciate her excuses.

> *With increased maturity and wisdom, each personality will begin to function more and more in strengths and less in exaggerated weaknesses.*

The opposite of the workaholic is the Phlegmatic who—given a choice—wouldn't do anything that takes exertion. By nature he has less innate energy than the other personalities and has a limited quantity of self-motivation. He will be pleasant and smiling, and the others seem to like him best. He seems to have no obvious faults.

"Remember that these illustrations are somewhat caricaturized, showing how the personalities are likely to function when they are out of balance—when their weaknesses are more prominent than their strengths," I reminded our class. "Of course, with increased maturity and wisdom, each personality will begin to function more and more in strengths and less in exaggerated weaknesses.

"Once you get a feel for the different personalities, you'll have a new gift of discernment and understanding that is more valuable than a personal psychiatrist—and you won't have to grab for your BlackBerry!"

I asked Rose to come up and bring a chart we had prepared for this session. She asked the class, "Many people feel stuck in

26

a 'workhouse' rather than a workplace. Have you ever felt that way?"

"Yes!" answered several voices.

"When Florence and I decided to give this class and began organizing the stories you'll hear later, we both realized that our topic is really about one simple thing that seems to be missing not only in the workplace but other places as well: *kindness.*" Rose set up the chart as she spoke.

"When we don't understand others it's hard to be kind to them." She continued. "Knowing the different personalities and their natural gifts can be an invaluable workplace tool in helping us lead, serve, or work with understanding and kindness alongside others.

"I know a few of you have already read *Personality Plus* and understand the basic differences in the four temperaments: *Sanguine, Choleric, Melancholy,* and *Phlegmatic.* We'll get into more detail as the weeks go by. But for now remember this: each personality has its own natural strengths that will complement those of someone who has the opposite personality."

In the workplace—whether a large corporation, a small company, or even a home office—knowing that the personalities are meant to support one another is crucial to kindness, happiness, and the definition of success, which, according to the dictionary, is "achieving a favorable and desired result."

"Don't we all want that?" Rose asked, and pointed to the chart at the front of the room.

How the Four Personalities Can Contribute to Success at Work

Popular Sanguine: An extroverted optimist who makes life fun

Powerful Choleric: An extroverted leader who takes charge easily

Perfect Melancholy: An introverted pessimist who may be prone to genius

Peaceful Phlegmatic: An introverted mediator who rolls with life's punches

"You don't have to agree with others, enjoy them, or even respect them, especially since some haven't yet earned that respect," I explained, taking over from Rose. "But to live and work harmoniously and productively in life, you *do* have to know how to appreciate others and be kind to them. My mother used to call it manners.

"So if you want to be a successful businessperson in whatever organization you are working, you'll have to practice some common courtesy by taking a little time to understand people: how they see the world differently from you, what emotional needs they have, and how you can best help them bring their natural gifts to the table, *not* how you can shape them into little mini-clones of you," I told our class.

"Mini-clones! Ha! That's funny!" said Holly Homes.

"Hilarious!" Howard agreed.

I laughed, too, but not wanting the Sanguines to take over the class—which they *will* do, given the chance—I quickly continued.

"No matter the type of business or the age of the people working there, the personalities will always show up in the way the people think and act. One area where the influence of personalities is easily seen is in the way people dress."

Sanguines are bright, fun, the life of the party, and they show off better than they show up. Their clothes and behavior are meant to be noticed. They are often shocking and loud. Sometimes they think bad attention is better than no attention at all.

Cholerics are born leaders and quickly decisive. They don't like to be told what to do or what to wear and may respond in shock to rules they believe are rigid or restricting. This is their way of taking charge.

Melancholies are deep, thoughtful, and introspective. They feel outward dress is a way to express their creativity without

28

saying a word. Melancholies come in two types: the perfect, buttoned-up, professional look or the free-spirited, artsy, intellectual style.

Phlegmatics are easygoing, pleasant, and friendly. They love the word *casual* and, if they could, would come to work in their pajamas. In fact, some current adolescent daytime fashions *are* T-shirts with pajama bottoms! Be careful—the boss may send you home to take a long nap.

"That's true!" said Carmen, the high school teacher. "A lot of my students come dressed as if they just rolled out of bed. To them it's 'cool.'"

Don't Try to Change Others

Rose reminded the class how her mother had tried to change her into a Melancholy. "Don't try to change others. It will frustrate you and annoy them!"

If you think of the opposite personalities as being two sides of the same coin, then you'll understand that we will naturally be drawn to those who complement us, our opposites.

We see this in marriages. We tend to fall in love with someone who fills in our weaknesses. If you understand this and can be grateful for these differences, then as you fill in each other's gaps, you'll have a happy, well-rounded family. If, on the other hand, you put your efforts into changing your mate—or your children—trying to "shape them up," you may have a disappointing life. By knowing the personalities, you'll see the differences in others as pluses and you won't spend your life waiting for them to change and become wonderful like you. It rarely happens.

The same is true in the workplace. Wishing that someone in your workplace would change will keep you stuck in a miserable mode. If you try to reshape your co-workers, you will probably be frus-

Brilliance in being the boss or a respected employee comes in recognizing others' strengths and weaknesses and helping others shine.

trated in your home away from home. You can modify other people's behavior at work, but you'll have trouble changing their natural reactions.

At home and in the office, we're drawn together by our different strengths, but it's bossiness, selfishness, fear, and laziness—our weaknesses—that will drive us apart. Brilliance in being the boss or a respected employee comes in recognizing others' strengths and weaknesses and helping others shine. Effective team members don't just tolerate each other; they genuinely respect—and don't resent—the different gifts that everyone brings to the office family.

The Value of People

"I used to think everyone needed to change to be like me," said Rose. "The study of the personalities has taught me to counter what our culture currently promotes: *that people are basically useful or not useful.* We've reduced people into things. As Harry S Truman once said, 'It's amazing what you can accomplish if you do not care who gets the credit.'"

The class seemed to relate to that and listened as Rose continued.

"As a Choleric employer, I admit that I've hired people in the past based primarily on how much they could produce for me. While production certainly is necessary (I do like to eat and I like to shop), it's not a human being's primary purpose. *Each person is unique, unrepeatable, and worthy of love and respect.* Each of us is a gift to our family, our workplace, and our community. Understanding the unique giftedness of the other personalities has helped me see that *people are valuable whether they are productive or not.* No matter how big or small, how young or old, we must remember that people *do* things; they *are not* things.

"I've also been working in ministry with divorced men, women, and their children, and I've found that our culture's utilitarian attitude that *makes us use and discard others is what causes marriages to end, families to break up, and formerly successful companies to fail*," she finished.

But when the different personalities feel appreciated (Sanguine), safe (Phlegmatic), valued (Melancholy), and respected (Choleric), they *will* produce their best fruits! You can count on that.

The Most Important Thing

As the session neared an end, I came up to the front of the room and shared a story we'd received from Choleric-Sanguine Betsy, who had been teaching her family the personalities and was asked to give a presentation at a Mother's Day event at her church.

Knowing that every speaker should carefully plan her talk, Betsy decided to ask her adult children what she'd done as their mother that most positively impacted their lives. Betsy was sure they would name many of the loving sacrifices that mothers make, but their answer surprised her.

"The personalities, Mom," came the unanimous reply from her three children. They shared that knowing their own temperament, and how to tell those of others, helped them at school with their teachers, at college, and on the job in their current careers.

There had been some surprises along the way as well. Betsy's Melancholy son, Brandon, had always picked on and criticized his silly Sanguine sister, Laura. When Betsy warned that it was likely he might end up marrying a complementary Sanguine, he was aghast! *Never*, he thought.

One day he came to his mother and admitted, "Mom, after you said I might marry a Sanguine, I started looking around at all the girls I like at school. They're *all* Sanguine!"

Parents are the first leaders in our lives, and their primary task is *not* to insure our fun, secure our comfort, or provide for all our needs. Their job is to prepare us for life. And knowledge of the personalities is a time-tested and powerful tool to teach our kids— or our company personnel—so they will learn how to appreciate and get along with others for the benefit of all.

Success is not so much about power, control, or personal gain as it is being able to recognize, respect, and receive the gift of others, whether they are like you or not.

"What's our topic next session?" asked Fran. Then she muttered, "Darn! I can't seem to find my course materials. They were right here a minute ago!"

Rose replied, "Next week Florence will share some hilarious stories about her children and how they were *born* with their personalities. See you then."

"Here are Fran's papers. She left them under her jewelry brochures."

It was Dr. Hastings. He'd been waiting all day to see if Fran would ever notice she'd left them behind. Melancholies usually have the answers, but they won't give them until they are asked.

What Did We Learn This Time?

- People are productive, but they are not things to be used.
- Don't try to change other people; change your own understanding of them.
- Learn to appreciate the Sanguine's light touch.
- Learn to appreciate the Choleric's take-charge energy.
- Learn to appreciate the Melancholy's attention to detail.
- Learn to appreciate the Phlegmatic's faithful support.
- Everyone—no matter how frustrating—has natural strengths that can benefit *your* business.

2

You're Born with Your Personality

"I've got the class today," I (Florence) reminded Rose.

She responded in typical Sanguine fashion: "Great! I'll be happy to sit in the back and listen to your stories. I never get tired of them."

"Well, *that's* a relief!" We both laughed. "I'll call you up to share some of your stories today, too." Moments later, we were happy to see the group arrive on time, and so I started with a question. "Does anyone know where we get our personality?"

It's a question raised in every class. We want to know where we came from, where we are going, and what's happening to us in between. These are questions that have been asked throughout the ages, so we'll handle one of these today and show you that you're born with your personality.

In my lifelong love of teaching, I've found that pupils learn best when the teacher is excited about the material and can prove the subject through her own experience. That's certainly been true for me in teaching the personalities. When I studied the ancient Greek philosopher Hippocrates and his writings as a physician on the four temperaments, it changed my marriage to Fred so much that we began to teach other couples what we had learned. Then we applied the principles to our children and later to our grandchildren.

Over and over again we've seen the truth that we're all born with a dominant personality. My daughter Lauren's three sons are good examples: low-key, inoffensive, and pleasant Phlegmatic Randy; chatty, humorous Sanguine showman Jonathan; and Bryan, a strong, controlling Choleric leader. Now we enjoy our new crop of grandchildren, who continue to teach us that we are born with our own personality.

Recently we had a family from Paris in our home. The parents could speak English, but the two young boys—ages seven and eleven—could not. Our seven-year-old Lianna, my son Fred's daughter, knew the little boy could not understand her, so they both gestured, smiled, patted, and pointed. Within minutes they were holding hands and gazing into each other's eyes. Lianna, with her deep, sensitive Melancholy spirit, didn't need words to fall in love with the romantic French boy who kissed her in the backseat of the van. Meanwhile, Lianna's four-year-old brother, Jack, was talking away to the older French boy, unaware that he didn't know a word Jack was saying as he politely nodded and smiled. Sanguines don't care if you understand them as long as you let them talk and just keep smiling.

Here were four children, true to their own personalities, communicating effectively with new friends who didn't even speak the same language. The people who come in and out of your business or work environment will speak different languages, too, but by studying the personalities, you'll be able to better understand them. (And if not, you can just smile and nod.)

"Our focus today is that each one of us was born with a personality—not as empty little tablets waiting for life to write the script," I said, then asked Rose to come up and share some of her examples.

34

"I was always aware of the differences in personalities between my brothers and sisters, even when they were infants, but I didn't know why we weren't all alike," she said. "I remember vividly that I actually enjoyed doing dishes after dinner and mopping the kitchen floor to make it shine. But others in my family would hide in the bathroom until chore time was over. I know now that Cholerics like work. They see the mess in life and take great pride in cleaning, fixing, and brightening it up. It makes them feel valuable, and then they look around for other chores to do.

"Years later I saw the same thing when I was stepmother to little Choleric Mikey. When he was at our home for the weekends, my sister's Phlegmatic son, Joe, who was close to Mikey's age, would also come stay with us. They grew up like brothers, with Mikey telling Joe what to do and Joe usually doing it.

"But one day I asked them to stay inside and not to go into the backyard since the lawn had been recently reseeded. When they thought I wasn't looking, they willfully disobeyed and ran outside anyway. I knew I had to discipline them. I'm sure it was Mikey's idea, but Joe followed. I called them in and scolded them. 'That's it! I've had it. You two will be doing chores all afternoon!' I said. I assigned Joe Windex duty for all the glass tables in the house and sent Mikey to clean the bathroom.

"A few minutes later I noticed Joe was slumped over, sad-faced and hating the work, pushing the paper towels around on the glass tabletop slowly and dramatically, as if the whole world needed to see how miserable he was. But from down the hall I heard the sound of Mikey cheerfully whistling the *Pink Panther* theme. When I walked in the bathroom, he was working away, scrubbing the toilet, wiping the counter, and cleaning the mirrors. He was happy! *This will not do as discipline*, I thought. I remembered that Cholerics hate to sit around and do nothing, so I sent him to his room, told him to sit on the bed, and forbade him to play with any toys, read any books, or even rearrange the bedcovers. Just sit there. He hated it.

"And Phlegmatic Joe? Well, I let him continue to polish every glass surface in the house until he was exhausted. Phlegmatics get tired easily. I had learned a lesson: *you can't effectively parent your children when you don't know your children.* For discipline you don't need to hurt them—just assign them a task their personality doesn't like to do."

We Cannot Change Our Stripes

When Rose finished, I brought this concept back to the workplace: the people in your business didn't become the way they are overnight. Like the children in our families, they were born that way. It doesn't take long for a parent to realize that not all children act alike, but seldom do we know what to do with each one—the peaceful, easygoing one; the moody, tearful one; the bubbly, into-everything one; and the one who may be trying to run your entire household from her crib.

Some Like Things Plain

Unless we are forcibly changed by extreme adverse circumstances, we will always have the strengths—and some of the weaknesses—of our inborn personality. My son Fred is a perfect Melancholy. When he was about five, he got up early one morning and, when I came into the kitchen, was coming in from the patio. I asked cheerfully, "Hi, Fred. How are things going for you today?"

He answered in a heavy tone, "All right so far. I haven't run into any people yet." He knew "people" would come with the day, but at least he'd been spared up until now.

In his room I had put up an awning and a striped bedspread to match. As a mother I've never believed children should grow up in plain white rooms; they should all have a theme. Each bedroom in our house represented a nationality of our heritage, and Fred's was the courtyard of a German castle. The carpet on the floor looked like bricks, and the walls were plastered to look like stone.

When my friends would come over with little children, I'd let them play in Fred's room with his toys while he was at school. Before he came home, I'd try to straighten up the room so he wouldn't know I'd let anybody in there. I'd pat down the bed, fluff up the pillows, and set Raggedy Andy against the wall. This doll wore a custom suit that matched the bedspread. I was really into extreme decorating.

But from the beginning, Fred was into details and could spot problems from a distance. When he came home, he'd go to his room and come out depressed. He'd say to me, "You've had people in my room again." His accusing tone would make me defensive.

"How do you know?"

"The bedspread stripes are crooked, the pillows aren't the way I left them, and Andy is on his face." He always knew every detail of his room.

As a teenager he didn't appreciate me. "You know what's wrong with you?" he'd ask, as I looked shocked. "You think you're funny."

I'd respond joyfully, "And aren't we glad! If it weren't for my sense of humor, we wouldn't live in this big house." He'd groan and go to his room.

Fred has never changed. This week we were standing together in the living room of a house I've lived in and now want to rent out. As he looked at my castle decor, my two-story wall up the stairs totally covered with well-framed pictures of my life, and the Cabbage Patch dolls on the ledge, he sighed.

"This will all have to be taken down. No one wants the glitter and the dolls and pictures of you. They just want it all white. We've all gotten used to your style of decorating and we like it, but renters want it just plain. Yes, just plain."

So now my job is to "plain" down my house. My Melancholy son is right. Renters won't want my decorating; they just want it plain! I'll paint the whole house basic white. They won't like the large three-by-four-foot framed picture of a wide-eyed frog in the bright green powder room; they may not find the sweeping eyelashes amusing and may not appreciate the caption: "Emphasize your best feature." I laugh every time I see my frog, but *they* may not think it's funny. Renters just want it plain. Yes . . . just plain.

Funerals Are Fun

Think about your children. Do some of them want their life "just plain" but you've been trying to decorate their days? It takes time for people to learn to minimize the weaknesses of their personality and maximize their strengths. This is especially important for harmony in the workplace. As children, though, we do not always realize that the ideas and tendencies that seem natural to us may not be appreciated by others.

My oldest daughter, Lauren, was mostly Choleric with a bonus of 50 percent Melancholy. It was going to be her way and, if you didn't follow, she'd go into a noticeable depression. She obeyed all the school rules and was the teacher's pet, so she had no problem being the room monitor and turning in children who'd misbehaved.

Second-born Marita was Sanguine—let's make school fun! She was frequently in some sort of trouble and never let me know when the parent-teacher meetings were scheduled. Her sincere aim in education was to keep Mother away from the teachers.

Marita and her Sanguine cousin, Dwayne, had given fits all year long to the sixth-grade teacher, Mr. Hamilton. No matter how I warned or threatened them, they would come home each day to tell of another daring trick they'd pulled on poor Mr. Hamilton. On the last day of school they came home joyful and announced, "We killed him!"

"You killed whom?" I asked.

"Mr. Hamilton. He dropped dead right in front of us in the classroom." There they were, jumping up and down and taking

38

credit for his demise. Naturally I thought this was another one of their Sanguine exaggerations until Lauren came home mournful and teary.

"Did you hear the terrible news? Mr. Hamilton is dead."

"Really dead?" I asked. "Like *dead*-dead?"

She thought a minute while I processed the news and then she added, "I guess I'll have to collect money for flowers and make a list of all the kids who want to go to the funeral."

"Can we go?" Marita asked.

Dwayne shouted from the kitchen as he stood staring into the open refrigerator, "I've never even been to a funeral. That will be fun!"

Lauren did organize the classroom good-byes, and Marita and Dwayne—who finally got a touch of reality—went quietly to the funeral, feeling appropriately sorry that Mr. Hamilton was *dead*-dead.

The Impact of Personality

So we need to accept the fact that we will not always appreciate the personalities of others, and they will not always find ours to their liking. In addition, we need to accept that we can't change others—but we can make some changes in ourselves. We can work at diminishing the weaknesses of our personality so that our strengths can come to the fore.

No matter what our personality is, it impacts how we approach a team meeting, company council, church picnic, or even a corporate event.

The Popular Personality—Sanguine

"Sanguines have trouble getting anywhere on time. Amazing things happen to them that don't happen to others, and their exciting stories make great excuses for their lateness," I told the class.

"Sanguines think everyone should enjoy their laughable mistakes, but the Cholerics write them off as stupid, they depress the Melancholies, and the Phlegmatics are just glad that no one is upset with *them*."

Holly Homes agreed. "Boy, Florence, you're right about that! What's the big deal about being a little late anyway? People should learn to lighten up!"

Choleric Darlene shot back, "When you show up . . . we'll lighten up!" She wasn't laughing, but she must have realized how hard she sounded and smiled. Holly rolled her eyes. I quickly continued the lesson.

"You might think twice about letting the Sanguine bring the refreshments for your company party. They would do better decorating than planning the details. They love to buy ornaments, streamers, figurines, confetti, and special napkins—but may forget where they put them. How often have I bought discount Santa Claus napkins after Christmas only to find them in a cupboard after the next Christmas? To help me remember where things are, I set aside one cabinet for holiday decorations, placemats, centerpieces, and special dishes."

Aside from the tendencies to lose things and forget where we put them, we Sanguines have a very poor estimation of how long it will take us to do anything. We think we can do everything quickly, but then something goes wrong and we arrive late at the meeting we're running, and we are a visible wreck. I had to learn to leave home a half hour earlier than necessary, and even then I was just about on time and often still late.

Sanguines tend to spend more time on the decorations than the details.

If you are a Sanguine, recall your childhood days and review the funny things you did and how you got into trouble. How have these things been carried into your current behavior? If you are asked to be responsible for an event in your workplace, realize you must get organized ahead of time, not plan anything too difficult, pick up props the day before, and leave for the event early. Even though you have the natural charm to cover up problems and the innate ability to make occasions fun, don't push your luck. Surprise your co-workers and be early!

The Powerful Personality—Choleric

Cholerics are too busy to take on anything as trivial as holiday parties at the office and should assign others to do it. They are probably already representing the company at cancer drives and charity balls—so they should hire a caterer. "Don't try to make pumpkin pies for the Thanksgiving party," I warned. "Let someone else do the cooking."

As a Choleric child with a Phlegmatic mother, it was easy for me to take over. Mother was overworked and tired and I could do two days' work in one. Besides having excess energy I learned early to take control of situations and people, become the leader, and delegate the things I didn't like to do.

One year Marita and I were invited to join a charity mother-daughter group that was going to instill "the art of giving" to our children. That Christmas we were to make lovely cookies for some hospital. But after Marita spilled the whole bowl of batter into the open silverware drawer, we both gave up.

Then I had an idea. I was scheduled to leave town the day we were supposed to turn in our hospital cookies. I was to speak at a mother-daughter banquet, so I prevailed on a friend, who had two girls in the charity group, to make a dozen extra cookies that would be from Marita and me. She agreed, so I left town feeling everything was under control.

Seeing me pause, Fran Taylor piped up with, "Yep! We Cholerics want control as long as we can find others to do the work! I love to delegate. I'm good at it!"

41

I was happy to see the group was getting it, and I continued with my story.

"At the banquet I regaled the ladies with my cookie failure. The whole thing was funny until I got home the next day and received a call from the Melancholy cookie chairman, who told me my cookies were of such poor quality that the cookie committee had convened and voted to reject my entry. Reject the Christmas cookies I hadn't even made? I knew my friend had probably baked three dozen delicious, decorated cookies, but she'd left town for the holidays."

To save face, I quickly baked a fresh batch of cookies, iced them, sprinkled them with red candies, and drove them over to this dour woman's home. I showed the chairman the platter of new cookies and said, "I'm so sorry. Here are some much better cookies. I know you won't serve the old ones and I'll be happy to take them back home. The kids will be glad to eat them. So give me the bad ones, and I'll give you these."

The Melancholy chairman's face grew red. "Just a minute, I'll be right back." I followed her a little way and stood outside the kitchen where I heard her smashing my cookies into little pieces. She came back out and handed me my plate of crumbs. I later learned she'd found out that I had "cheated" and not made my own cookies—against the group's rules! So to punish me, she'd refused to serve the cookies and had been delighted to call me to tell me they'd been "rejected." Marita and I "unjoined" the Charity League and haven't ever made cookies together again.

The Cholerics should skip the small stuff and just run for governor.

"So, you Cholerics, think of when you agreed to do too much and got yourself into trouble," I told the class. "Don't agree to make the cookies for the party—delegate. Stay within your time constraints and you won't be rejected. Save your talent for something at which you excel. Give the commencement address, or run for governor."

The Perfect Personality—Melancholy

Melancholies are the ones that your children's teachers all hoped would be classroom volunteers. Before I married Fred, I was a high school drama and English instructor. As a Choleric-Sanguine teacher, I wanted *only* Melancholy helpers. They did the job on time and they did it perfectly—even though they went home depressed because a child broke their crystal cake plate.

Since our natural personalities never change, if you are a former classroom helper, you are probably still functioning in that capacity in your workplace. Even though you tend to be a little shy, we appreciate that you volunteer and save the rest of us from our disasters. We need you. You will plan ahead, frost the cupcakes, sprinkle silver dragées on top, arrive early with the cakes on a silver platter, and pour punch from a matching silver pitcher into crystal goblets. You will be dressed appropriately—never gaudy and *never* with spots on your skirt! You may even anticipate the very worst that could happen and have enough foresight to bring a replacement apron, an item of clothing that is almost foreign to the opposite Sanguine.

You will speak softly and kindly and make sure everything is done perfectly, not like the Sanguine who came late and flustered or the Choleric who didn't come at all but sent caterers. And you still get

> *The Melancholies are ever ready, planning parties perfectly.*

depressed when your co-workers treat your best silver pitcher or crystal goblets carelessly.

"We don't mind that you need a day to stay home from work and recover from dealing with our disasters," I joked. "Come back to work when your headache is gone—we need you!"

The Peaceful Personality—Phlegmatic

If you are a Phlegmatic, be glad. You are the best-liked of all the personalities, and your calm attitude in a chaotic workplace is much appreciated. You don't get overly excited about anything, especially the office party. You don't care if the Sanguine was late, if the Choleric showed off by sending the caterer, or if the perfect Melancholy prepared a banquet.

When it's your turn, you'll do the best you can—and if that's not good enough, they can get someone else next year. You'll show up on time, bringing the Oreo cookies and whatever paper napkins you had on hand. If the flowery napkins are left over from last summer and today it's snowing, you'll just tell them to pretend they are in Florida. No one really cares. Your life is peaceful and you're not going to let one disastrous party get you down.

Your biggest problem will be if you have a covey of Cholerics who want you to shape up and make some *real* cookies from scratch. The answer to this is to assign them to bring the refreshments. Put them in charge of specific tasks and praise them a lot for whatever they do.

Everyone can relax when the balanced Phlegmatic is in charge.

Phlegmatics are usually good at that low-key, inoffensive way of convincing others in the office to do the work. Frenzied, scattered, or depressed employers could learn a thing or two from you!

Whether it's the office party or the daily routine in any workplace, the personalities will have an impact on how co-workers get the job done. When each personality is respected and people are appreciated for the strengths they bring to the task, it works best for all concerned. This means not only that workers' strengths are valued but that their weaknesses are overlooked as much as possible.

Your Childhood Can Give You a Clue

Remember that personality traits are inborn. Think back to when you were a child and see how much you are still the same today. Did you have a parent like you? A Sanguine parent can't handle a child who is Melancholy and gets easily disheartened over minor failure. Nor the opposite; the perfect Melancholy parent is often baffled by the Sanguine's frivolity and silly sense of humor.

Similarly, the Choleric parent with a million things to do wonders why the Phlegmatic child needs to be pushed to get his room cleaned up or why she steps over those toys instead of picking them up.

"The Phlegmatic parent can't understand why anyone cares how the house looks. She's happy to have a Choleric child who likes to do housework and run errands," I said, pleased with how our class had sat and listened so well to the presentation.

As we wound up the session and the group started leaving for the day, Dr. Hastings stayed behind and asked if we could talk for a few minutes. "I don't normally talk about these things, Florence, but this personality study has hit some nerves with me, and . . . well, I feel that I can trust you."

"Go ahead, Doctor. I'm listening."

"I see now that my mother was a hard-driving Choleric—no offense—who pushed me into medical school. It's not that I didn't like medicine, but I'd had a dream of going to foreign countries and helping the poor. A missionary had come to our church one Sunday, and those sad little faces he showed us on the overhead projector made me almost cry. I wanted to help somehow."

"Well, that's a typical response from a caring and sensitive Melancholy. Whatever happened to your dream?"

"I remember asking Mother if we could send some money to the missions and she said no, we needed to save money for my college because she thought I should be a doctor. 'When you're a doctor you can help a *lot* of people, Charles,' she said. After my residency I seriously thought about being a missionary doctor, but Mother again protested. 'You'll never make money that way,' she said and suggested I take a trip to some poor country for a month and then come back to my practice."

I asked him if he'd done that.

"No, but Mother is proud of me anyway because I did become a doctor and I've made more money than my brother ever did."

I offered him my own motherly support, being careful not to be too pushy or too glib.

"Charles, I'm sure your mother appreciates you in many ways. I'm sure no one taught her to understand your Melancholy heart, but I do. That's the gift that comes with knowing the personalities." I could see him relax, and he smiled.

"I guess each personality has its own unique emotional needs, too, right?"

"Emotional needs. Yes! And that's exactly what we'll cover in our next class."

What Did We Learn This Time?

- People don't come into the world as blank slates.
- Everyone has natural strengths and weaknesses—everyone!
- Each personality is motivated differently.
- Your childhood holds clues to your workplace personality.

3

The Emotional Needs
of Personalities

I (Rose) was glad to see Florence spending time with Dr. Hastings in the back of the room before class began. We could both tell that something had been bothering him, something deep that had probably been there for many years. Despite his many degrees and initial arrogant manner, Charles seemed drawn to Florence's strong, motherly wisdom. Studying the personalities requires that we look inside ourselves, and that can bring up old emotional wounds. I know.

I looked around at the rest of the men and women in our class.

Carmen Gonzalez—our Perfect Peaceful—was coming out of her shell. Clearly Howard "Johnson" had eyes for *her* big brown eyes. He'd told me at the afternoon break last time that she'd offered to help him with his latest diet plan. She was good with charts and graphs and was going to come up with a way for him to count daily calories. I hoped he'd succeed, but I knew if I worked at a restaurant I'd be eating all day long! He was good for her. He made her laugh and feel appreciated. She gave him the attention that other women might not. I wondered if they saw each other outside the classroom.

Sanguine-Phlegmatic Holly had been flirting with Phlegmatic Pastor Paul, but he didn't seem too interested. I'm sure he was scared.

Darlene still bossed Hans around. Every week she told him where they would sit. I'm surprised he didn't ask her permission to go to the bathroom.

Fran Taylor was right . . . she did like to tell others what to do. No wonder she held an upper-level position at her company. But I wondered if people thought she was too pushy. Did anyone ever tell her how much they appreciated her hard work?

All the people in our group were just like everyone else in the world: hungry for love and starving for affection, affirmation, peace, or respect. Well, today we would help with *that*!

I asked the class, "What do you think is wrong with all of the unpleasant people in your workplace?"

"Nothing that a frontal lobotomy can't fix," said Dr. Hastings dryly.

Everyone roared.

"Now that's funny, Doc!" Howard exclaimed. I had to admit, it *was* funny. Maybe the doctor was feeling better after talking to Florence. She did have the magic touch in knowing how to meet the emotional needs of the personalities.

"Okay, let's settle down now. Thank you, Dr. Hastings. Remind me never to ask that question of a Harvard grad."

I explained to the group that there can be many reasons for unpleasant behavior, especially in the workplace. You don't have to be a psychologist to know that perhaps a person's emotional needs in childhood were never met and he or she is still behaving like an adult version of a first grader. Children eat to grow, but we may not realize that if their emotional needs are not fed, they will not grow up to be mature, balanced, and stable adults.

When kids are physically hungry, they begin to cry, scream, wilt, whine, wail, or worry. Their unmet needs often manifest in extreme behaviors. *The same thing happens with emotional hunger.* "If we were raised in a home with loving parents, minimum stress, and realistic affirmation of our abilities, our emotional needs were probably met and we were able to grow up to be well-balanced adults," I explained. "If, however, we were brought up by detached or uninvolved parents, by overly demanding parents, or with harsh discipline and/or physical or sexual abuse, we will attempt to fill the void we feel by pushing our personality strengths to extremes."

The room was silent. I knew we were touching on some tender spots, but I wanted to give them the *good news* about how to start meeting each other's needs at work—and at home—in healthy ways through understanding personalities.

Knowing the Emotional Needs

All people have a basic need to feel safe, valued, and loved. But each personality has its own particular set of emotional needs. In the workplace, understanding your personality needs as well as those of others makes harmony, productivity, and a happier atmosphere possible.

I put up the chart (see p. 50) so all could see. "This chart is in your printed materials as well," I pointed out. "Let's go over the basic emotional needs at work."

The Popular Personality—the Sanguine— Look at Me!

"Howard and Holly, let's start with the Sanguines: *you!*"

"Yay!" Holly cheered.

From the earliest days of childhood, Sanguines have a strong emotional need for attention and learn to do whatever it takes to

Basic Workplace Needs

Popular Sanguine *Basic desire:* fun	Powerful Choleric *Basic desire:* be in charge
Emotional needs: • attention • affection • approval	*Emotional needs:* • loyalty • achievement • appreciation
Cause of depression: • life/work no longer fun • no parties, no spending	*Cause of depression:* • life/work out of control • no business, no income
Stress relief: • moments of fun • eternal shopping	*Stress relief:* • detach from problem • start new project
How to help: • visit and give gifts • take him or her out to eat	*How to help:* • recognize effort • put him or her in charge
Peaceful Phlegmatic *Basic desire:* peace	**Perfect Melancholy** *Basic desire:* perfection
Emotional needs: • respect • feeling of worth • peace and quiet	*Emotional needs:* • order and perfection • sensitivity • silence and space
Cause of depression: • life/work not peaceful • no rest, no escape	*Cause of depression:* • life/work not perfect • no hope, no improvement
Stress relief: • watching television • rest and relaxation	*Stress relief:* • getting organized • time alone
How to help: • keep conflict down • respect his or her space	*How to help:* • listen to his or her problems • show warm concern

get it. If they draw attention by smiling, laughing, chattering, and entertaining, they will do these things. If their emotional needs aren't met with these behaviors, they will talk louder, yell, or cry. They may develop unhealthy ways to get people to notice them. If they are left alone, neglected, or abused, they carry into adulthood an insatiable desire for attention.

Look around your workplace. Is there someone who doesn't just walk in but makes an entrance? Someone who's loud in both action and dress? One who is a magnet for attention—wherever he or she may be. This person is hungry for "soul food": someone—or something—that can fill those emotional needs.

"Sanguines have innate charm, sense of humor, and conversational skills, but they can carry these to extremes by overdoing their looks and personality (*Don't you think I'm adorable?*), trying to attract attention by making a joke of everything, being unable to settle down, or babbling constantly," I said. "They can become overindulgent party animals who like to drink, smoke, eat, gamble, or shop too much."

"Okay, okay . . . I admit it!" Howard said as he patted his bulging belly and smiled. He liked being the center of attention.

Helping the Sanguine

What can you do for Sanguines gone to extremes? Since you are not a psychologist, it's not your job to be their personal counselor. In fact, you need to be careful of how involved you become. They have a strong emotional need for *affection*, loving to give it and get it. So you must be careful not to become too close. It's okay to compliment, notice new clothing or a hairstyle, praise tasks done right, and be gentle in correction. They need an abundance of *approval*, compared to others doing the same job, and will die for you if you say they did the best. "The Sanguines are desperate for *acceptance* into your favor or group," I concluded. "Make them feel they belong."

"Yes, please!" said Holly.

If You Are a Sanguine

What if you are a Sanguine? Reassess your emotional desires and make sure you don't behave like a child: no obvious seeking of attention, no asking for compliments, no whining or looking for pity, and no indulging in feelings of rejection. Aim to grow up—or shut up.

The Powerful Personality—the Choleric— Appreciate Me!

I switched gears to the next personality.

"Okay, Fran and Darlene, you're both mostly Choleric, so we're going to talk about you now!"

Darlene corrected me by adding, "I think I have Melancholy as a secondary."

"Yes, I think you do, too, and that's okay," I said. "Let's first focus on the Choleric." (I'm the teacher here!)

Cholerics know from childhood that they can do just about anything better than other people. Even if they were abused or put down in their efforts, they didn't quit but tried harder to show their ability. Often this makes them appear bossy, manipulative, and controlling. "Their zeal for life—considered a strength—gets carried to extremes in an effort to have others appreciate them," I explained. "Then they may spin out of balance and become a tyrannical workaholic."

"Like that swirling Tasmanian devil guy in the Warner Brothers cartoons!"

"Yes, Howard. Just like him."

Helping the Choleric

You can help Cholerics by putting them in charge of whatever they do well, but make sure they don't insult or degrade those assigned to their supervision. They need a *sense of control*; they need to know that you *appreciate* their hard work, that they have the *loyalty* of those they lead, and that they aren't talked about behind their back. They need to be in control without feeling their every move is being watched. If you train them to climb the ladder, they will be motivated to do more than you ask of them. Be open and honest—they can take it—and they will reward you.

If You Are a Choleric

"What if you are a Choleric?" I asked the class. "While you are anxious for *credit* for your *achievements*, be willing to do the work without asking for praise or pointing out how well you have done it. This behavior comes across as bragging and turns those both above and below you away from emotionally supporting you. A general needs the troops to be marching with him, not plotting mutiny."

"*Mutiny*! That's what I have to deal with *a lot*!" said Darlene in an exasperated tone.

I knew exactly what—and whom—she was talking about, so I told her, "Darlene, this is what is so great about knowing everyone's emotional needs. When you understand what others need—and give it to them—there will *be* no mutiny!"

I knew Darlene saw her husband as something of a wimp, but I hoped she would learn to step back and meet *his* needs, too, and allow him room to step up to the plate. Time would tell.

The Perfect Personality—the Melancholy— Understand Me!

"Now we come to the more introverted and reserved Melancholy, who usually does not like to be pointed out in the classroom, so Carmen and Dr. Hastings, we are *not* talking about you!" I grinned, and they both chuckled politely.

I knew that we'd had enough time in the last few weeks with our pleasant group that the Melancholies were feeling safe. While most Melancholies feel that no one will ever really understand them enough, I could see Carmen and Charles were open to hearing more about themselves.

"Melancholies want life to be perfect, and when parents are quarrelsome, fighting, embarrassing, or abusive, these children withdraw and create separate worlds for themselves where they can try to make an imaginary life. They may become antisocial. Sometimes this negative response leads to introspective writing, artistry, or poetry. And these deep, creative strengths can be carried to extremes in an effort to find emotional fulfillment," I said.

Whereas the extroverted Sanguine and Choleric are open and outspoken in their need for public affirmation, the introverted Melancholy is quiet and keeps his feelings hidden. People may often say, "I wonder what he's really thinking." The Melancholy needs to trust you and know you are for real before he or she will open up to you. They are suspicious and expect rejection. Their emotional needs are *sensitivity* and *support*, and therefore they are very easily hurt and will not thrive under a Sanguine boss who may be insensitive.

Melancholies may have come from families who looked at them as smart but no fun. Their parents tried to cheer them up but gave up and let them become loners. They work better by themselves and really want to think things through or do research on the subject. Not only do they get the point you are making, but they mull it over and wonder if there was some hidden meaning.

Helping the Melancholy

"To help Melancholies, let them know you are with them and affirm their worth and deep thinking. Say things like: 'You're right. I never thought of that,'" I told the class. "Melancholies will do the best for you if they feel you are supportive of their efforts. They need *space* and *silence* in their work area and don't wish to share their favorite pen with a Sanguine—who they know will forget to return it. Realize that they get easily discouraged and need you to pick them up without making light of their problems."

"Rose?" It was Carmen who had gently raised her hand. "What you just said is so true. But do you think Sanguines can really understand the sensitive nature of a Melancholy? The last man I dated was Sanguine, and while he was exciting to be with, he was always mocking me and making fun. I know he wasn't trying to be mean, but it hurt my feelings."

"Did you break up?" I asked. This was private stuff, but I sensed Carmen just needed to talk a little, and she seemed okay to speak in front of the others.

"Yes," she said, rather pitifully. "This may sound melodramatic, but I really do prefer the misery of loneliness over mockery."

I walked quietly over to Carmen, leaned down a bit, and lowered my voice. "Carmen, dear, yes . . . when Sanguines—or anyone else—make up their mind to meet your emotional needs, they will. I know, because I *am* a Sanguine. Maybe you just haven't met someone who really understands you!" I took a bold chance and looked over at Howard. "Right, Howie?" I grinned at him.

If You Are a Melancholy

What if you're a Melancholy? Understand that the office crew is too busy to affirm you constantly or try to pull you up from your moods. They expect you to be one of the gang, so try to join in and socialize. If someone borrows your pen, don't complain—just go get it back, smile, and say, "I'm saving you the trouble." Don't take everyone seriously and assume they are talking about you. Try to be a good sport and not be defensive. Help a Sanguine when you see him heading over a cliff of troubles. Don't stand by and watch him fall.

The Peaceful Personality—the Phlegmatic—Respect Me!

"Okay, we've saved the best for last!" I said. "Pastor Page and Hans . . . you're in the spotlight!"

Neither said a word, but they *did* smile.

When parents accept Phlegmatics for their easygoing nature and encourage whatever talent they have, they will develop normally. If, however, they are constantly compared unfavorably to a sibling or called a dummy in any way, they will withdraw and pretend to be happy alone. If this need for acceptance "as I am" is not fulfilled, they may quit and become low achievers. In an effort to find the peace they crave, their low-key strengths may be carried to passive extremes.

The emotional needs of the quiet, respectful Phlegmatics are *lack of stress* and a boost to their *feelings of low self-worth*. They long for peace and don't thrive in contentious situations. They may have come from a noisy family that didn't appreciate their need for peace and quiet and didn't affirm their occasional sense of humor. Phlegmatics have an excellent sense of right and wrong and an objective opinion on difficult office problems. They are natural counselors, as long as they don't get personally caught up in the problem.

Helping the Phlegmatic

Phlegmatics are faithful employees and balanced in nature. They will perform well for you if given a measure of *respect*. It is difficult for a Choleric to commend a Phlegmatic because, for them, praise is always connected to high levels of production. "Because Phlegmatics are quiet and don't brag, Cholerics don't think they are doing anything. Watch for whatever the Phlegmatic brings to the table in the way of team support," I suggested. "The Phlegmatic functions in subtleties—shades of gray—while the Choleric sees only dark black and bright white. No wonder these two don't understand each other."

I looked at Darlene and hoped she was listening.

If You Are a Phlegmatic

What if you're Phlegmatic? Accept the fact that your work group may not be people you would choose as best friends, but you are

56

one of them and they expect you to participate. You are the rock-solid balance and the moderator of the workplace; people will sense your wisdom and come to you for advice. Your family may have overlooked your quiet ability, but you will shine at work. "You are invited to the party—so join in!" I said. "Laugh with the Sanguine and give him a humorous response. Lift up the Melancholy and let her see you really care. Affirm the Choleric's activity and achievements."

I smiled at Hans and hoped he was listening, too.

When You Don't Know Someone's Emotional Needs

I could see that it was time to make the lesson stick, so I shared a personal story of how I had failed—miserably—in my own office when I did not understand this principle.

"Because of my personality, I've tended to fall into the trap of being on a mission (Choleric) to make everyone else have fun (Sanguine). Those are *my* emotional needs. But for a long time I didn't have a clue about the emotional needs of personalities in the workplace—or in any other relationships—and as a result I hurt some very special people," I said. "It was a long time ago and I hope, if they remember, that they have forgiven me."

It was the 1980s and I was so happily full of myself, I failed miserably as a leader of others. A decade earlier, the growing feminist movement had successfully engineered government assistance programs that encouraged women to own businesses. Since I was self-employed and owner of a small and growing real estate company, I decided to hire no one but women (sorry, guys!) to see if that might garner me even *more* special bureaucratic treatment. Oh-h-h, I should have known I was already headed down a slippery slope!

So I hired Kristi, an office manager who was a driven Choleric and conscientious Melancholy. She organized the front office, kept me on schedule, and tactfully refused to take any verbal abuse

57

from clients. Many women struggle to set and enforce boundaries at home or in the workplace, but Kristi was naturally gifted at graciously and appropriately saying no. I gave her lots of free rein and decision-making power. I knew enough not to micromanage her. We were both happy. So far, so good.

But then came Pam, a caring Phlegmatic with Melancholy sensitivity. She was a Little Person, definitely a minority, and since hiring minorities was all the rage, I was thrilled! I could outfit the office to accommodate Pam's special physical needs, and I would be even more of a special employer. What a great leader I was becoming! I took what I thought was a load off Kristi and assigned the incoming phone calls to Pam, along with some other detail work.

As the business flourished, I put an ad in the paper for more employees. Then I interviewed Sue, who was—oh, I could hardly stand the excitement—an African American! Yes! Another notch on my hiring-minorities belt. The Choleric power was going to my head as I became—at least in my own mind—the leader of a group of "special agents," formerly victimized women who would rise up and take over the world! I decided to give Sue lots of personal freedom and sent her into the field to drum up business.

And it gets better. One day Nance interviewed with me over lunch, and I hired her on the spot. Why? Because of her skills, work history, or personality? No. She was living a wild and unconventional lifestyle, and that was all I needed to complete my company. Nance would be the newest and most socially daring of all minorities at the time.

Now my ego had become so large that the outfitting of the doorways in our office wasn't only for the physically challenged! After a few months, however, my mission began to fail.

Kristi, a Choleric who naturally handled authority and decision making quickly and with great ease, was quietly (Melancholy) resenting that she could no longer direct and manage the clients who called in. In my own rash, Choleric mode—without asking or listening to Kristi—and thinking I'd done her a favor, I'd given the client calls to Phlegmatic Pam. Kristi's emotional needs were to be in charge and to feel that I understood her gifts and talents. She didn't mind hard work—she loved it. But I took it away.

Where Kristi thrived on telling demanding clients they could not talk to her or any of us "that way," Pam completely withered under the pressure. She'd get tongue-tied and nervous to the point of forgetting to write down the phone numbers or other important information. As a result, she didn't feel valuable to the office but inadequate. Being an introvert, Pam also seethed quietly and waited to see if things would change on their own. She didn't want to complain. And I had no idea that her emotional needs required that she be left alone to do her work well, away from chaotic clients.

Neither Kristi nor Pam felt they could come to me to ask for a change because I would quickly dismiss the problem or make suggestions on how they could improve their situation. I'd smile and cheer them up and offer to buy them lunch. And they'd smile, too, and go back to their quiet misery.

Like Pam, Sue was also a Phlegmatic with some Melancholy. She would have done anything I told her, faithfully and meticulously, but I sent her out alone into the field all day where she had to function as an extrovert with no clear guidance. She did well for a while, but it completely drained her. I'd projected my own emotional needs onto her: *Just give me the instructions and set me free. Don't try to manage me because I got it the first time and I'll be back when the job is finished.* That's what I did with Sue, thinking it would make her happy. But Sue worked best with the clear support of a Choleric to direct her. She's a natural team player, not a loner. She didn't have the energy or discipline to see the big picture, make a plan, and follow through all on her own. Her emotional needs were for someone to give her clear guidance and strong support. I just threw her to the lions.

And Nance? Well, she was an intense Melancholy-Phlegmatic who saw Sanguines as utterly insensitive, unreliable, and downright flaky. And I admit that now I understand why. I was oblivious to whatever personal struggles, along with those in the workplace, she or any of the other women in my office had.

I simply saw my role as briskly assigning tasks and cheering everyone up out of their funks. Not once did I ever sit down and ask any of these beautiful Melancholy women to share their hearts, their frustrations, or their dreams. I had no idea what they really needed from me. Nance never did trust me to give her any competent direction or instruction and as a result she did things her way, which was *not* the way our business needed to be run. The results were predictable.

Choleric-Melancholy Kristi, who needed to feel in charge, was hurt and angry that I'd taken her away from the job she liked. I thought, *Why couldn't she just adjust?*

Phlegmatic-Melancholy Pam, who needed peace, was overwhelmed and depressed. I wondered, *Why did she get so stressed over angry clients?*

Phlegmatic-Melancholy Sue, who needed strong direction, felt neglected and alone. I thought, *Why do I have to hold her hand?*

Melancholy-Phlegmatic Nance was distrusting and stubbornly stuck in doing things her way. I thought, *Why couldn't she see I was the boss?*

They were all miserable and so was I. All I wanted was a happy group of workers, and I didn't know what was wrong with them.

Finally, I admitted something needed to change. It was the day I realized Sue's personal belongings—little potted plant, pink calendar, and a framed photo of her young son in a baseball uniform—were still on her desk, but she hadn't been in the office for more than ten days! *Hmmm*, I thought, *she has a son?* I found out later that Sue had interviewed for another job in another city and had started working before I noticed she was gone. She probably had no

60

intention of ever coming back to get her things and to face me. Now that I think back, I remember we simply packaged up her items in a little cardboard box. Seven years later when we packed up our office to move to a new location, her box was still in our storage room.

Making Changes

"That's when I first read Florence Littauer's *Personality Plus* and heard that she'd be speaking at a conference in our state the next month," I told the class. "I shared an overview of the personalities with Kristi and Pam (the only women remaining in the office) and told them I'd pay for the trip to the conference. We all went and thoroughly enjoyed the event and all we learned. I was delighted to understand the personalities but mortified to admit I had completely ignored the natural gifts of the people in my office.

"For the first time I knew Kristi needed her authority back. When I restored her original assignments, she cheered up. I saw that Pam needed to stay quietly in the back room and crunch those numbers, which she did very well—without client conflict. But I had to remember she was there and go praise her often."

The Worst Things I Did as a Leader

As a Choleric I was trapped in my task-oriented, utilitarian view of others. I had reduced these precious people to "things"; they weren't women to me but office functions. With my new understanding of the personalities, I realized I had to be careful not to continue to reduce them to Melancholies or Phlegmatics. I had to see them as whole persons, each woman valuable not for *what she did* but for *who she was*.

As a Sanguine I was totally ignorant of their need for understanding and sensitivity instead of jokes and free lunches. Their emotional needs had gone unmet.

61

The Best Things I Did as a Leader

"I came to appreciate that I had hired only Melancholies," I continued, "perhaps knowing at some deep level that Sanguines always need their balance, someone to fill in their weaknesses. I also admitted that all my Sanguine lightheartedness and playful 'encouragement' could not—and maybe even *would* not—make them happy. In fact, my attitude might actually set their hearts in stone. They needed to know that I truly listened and cared about them, not just their productivity.

I had to see them as whole persons, each woman valuable not for what she did but for who she was.

"Also, I sought out knowledge from someone smarter than me who could lead me to a better place of understanding. The personalities have changed my life and have helped me be able to love and lead others in the way that's best for them—not me."

Kristi stayed with me for seventeen years and then left to go into her own business. Recently I ran into her at a restaurant, and she and I reminisced fondly about our years together.

Pam moved to Florida after she met (and later married) a handsome man at the annual Little People's Convention in Las Vegas. Maybe he listened to her!

"Now I'm teaching personalities to help others in their workplace," I said, and looked out at our group. "Are you like I was? Are you on a well-intentioned quest for power or success that is really doomed from the start because you have your focus on productivity instead of on the people who work for you?

"Maybe it's time to see that businesses are ultimately about individual people with unique personalities and distinct emotional needs. Continuing to ignore these needs sets you up for a mission that's, well, impossible!"

I smiled. "Okay, thanks everyone. Our next session will cover all the different ways the personalities try to control each other.

Like how Choleric Florence has tried to control me by telling me I have to teach the next class. So, once again, I am willing to sacrifice and be servant-hearted . . ."

Businesses are ultimately about individual people with unique personalities and distinct emotional needs.

"Wait!" Howard said. "*You're* not Melancholy!"

"Or Phlegmatic!" Pastor Paul said.

Everyone laughed out loud. They were getting it!

Holly chimed in, "Yeah, we Sanguines are good at just pretending to be all those things, right?"

"Right!" everyone said in unison.

What Did We Learn This Time?

- Every personality has distinct emotional needs.
- Unmet emotional needs can change natural strengths into weaknesses.
- Sanguines need you to notice and compliment them.
- Cholerics need you to appreciate all that they do for you.
- Melancholies need you to understand and not ridicule them.
- Phlegmatics need you to respect who they are, regardless of how much they do.

4

Personality Nuances

"Rose, you seem so sure of yourself in knowing people's personalities. *Have you ever been wrong?*" Dr. Charles Everett Hastings III—the Perfect Melancholy—was looking right at me with his steely blue-gray eyes. The room was silent and all eight students were staring at me.

"Why, yes, Dr. Hastings," I (Rose) gulped. "As a matter of fact I *have* been wrong."

So I told the class the story of when I was stepmother to then-four-year-old Mikey and had completely misdiagnosed his natural temperament. I loved him as my own and wanted to have some special connection with him since we had no genetic ties. His mother was Choleric-Melancholy, and his father was Phlegmatic-Melancholy. Mikey was sparkly, outgoing, and full of energy, so I began to convince him, his father, and myself that he was Sanguine—like me!

But one Sunday morning, I saw him in the bathroom getting ready for church. He was trying to perfect that little wave in his hair and was almost in tears trying to get it just right. "It's okay, honey," I said. "You look very handsome!" But Mikey didn't seem to hear me.

A few days later I asked him to clean up his room, and later I realized it had been quiet in there for an unusually long time. I walked in and saw him lining up all his model cars in perfect order on the carpeted floor, spacing each one exactly the same distance apart, and arranging them in color as well. Then he looked the line over and decided to readjust each one again, unaware of the long time he'd been spending in perfecting his project. I stood there struck with the ego-shattering reality I could no longer avoid: *Mikey was Melancholy!*

As soon as I was open to the truth, memories came flooding in that made me realize I'd not seen his natural temperament because I wanted him to be a personality that pleased me. In doing that, I'd failed to appreciate the gift of who he really was. His high energy level wasn't Sanguine but Choleric—the other outgoing extrovert of the four temperaments. That night at dinner I made an apologetic announcement and shared my observations with my Melancholy-Phlegmatic husband and Melancholy-Choleric stepson. "You're free now, Mikey, to be who God made you!" And then—true to my Sanguine nature—I rolled my eyes humorously and made them both laugh when I said, "And please, dear God, help me survive being the only Sanguine in the house!"

"That's how I felt growing up!" said Howard.

"*Me, too!*" added Holly. But then she thought about it for a minute and added, "Well, I guess I did have another Sanguine brother . . ."

Sometimes Sanguines even forget their siblings.

"Remember," I told the class, "a slapdash analysis of yourself or others can cause deep resentments and ruin the relationship . . . and the work environment. So if you're not sure of someone's personality, don't assume. Keep observing and keep learning. Just knowing the basics of the four personalities won't be enough. If you don't study some of the nuances of the personalities, you may easily mistake yourself—or someone else—for the wrong temperament. And that can cause more trouble than not knowing the personalities at all."

In this session, we're giving you some of the more important underlying principles to remember in identifying and working with the personalities. They'll also help when *you* take the Personality Profile test in the appendix of this book. Florence and I want this book to be your office desktop guide, so consider the following a quick and easy reference of some personality nuances.

There Is No Superior Personality

People might get the idea that one or more of the four personalities are superior to the others. But that competitive attitude disregards the importance and value that all four personalities bring to the human family.

I asked our class if they had ever studied the human heart in high school biology. Two of the chambers (I forgot the names, but Dr. Hastings reminded me they are the right atrium and right ventricle) receive blood from the body and send it to the lungs for air. Then the other two chambers (left atrium and left ventricle) send the freshly oxygenated blood back out to the body. All four chambers constantly work together in regular rhythm—*receive, return, receive, return*—and that's what gives life to the human body.

"I get it," said the doctor. "These four personalities working together will be the life of your workplace. They will be the heart of your company!"

"Thank you, Dr. Hastings. I couldn't have said it better myself."

- Two personalities tend to be receptive by taking things inward (Melancholy and Phlegmatic). They tend to keep thoughts and feelings inside, usually until trust is built or to avoid

66

unnecessary conflict. Some call them the easygoing Type B, the tortoise of Aesop's fable *The Tortoise and the Hare*. We call them introverts.

- The other two personalities are more active at moving and pushing outward (Choleric and Sanguine). They are often quick to share too much information and may even shove it down your throat. Some call them the hard-driving Type A, the hare in Aesop's race. We call them extroverts.

All four personalities are necessary in the workplace for sustaining a healthy and productive rhythm.

You Have Both Learned Behavior and a Default Mode

Depending on the circumstance, everyone learns to behave as necessary. All people can function in a quiet, introverted fashion—think classroom, courtroom, solemn religious service, or hospital room (*Sh-h-h-h-h!*). But to the introverts (Melancholy and Phlegmatic) this quiet reaction is the first response—their "default." It comes naturally.

Most people also know how to function as a take-charge person or loud extrovert in certain situations—think screaming at a football game, addressing a crowd, leading a meeting, or running the whole show (*Ladies and gentlemen, step this way!*)—but to the extroverts (Sanguine and Choleric) it's their default. It comes naturally.

What outward behaviors have you learned, and which really come naturally to you?

The Personalities Are Complementary

Opposites are meant to complement each other, completing together what the other naturally lacks. We know this about men and women, who are equal in dignity and value but different in gifts and strengths. Neither is superior, and the world needs both. If you read the list of Choleric strengths, they seem to indicate a

masculine bent (powerful, driven, risky,

Often personalities cross the gender lines for an even more interesting blend of people.

commanding, bold, and outspoken). Conversely, the Phlegmatic strengths appear to be *feminine* (kind, gentle, patient, careful, hidden, and soft-spoken). But temperaments don't determine your sex and your sex doesn't determine your temperament. Often personalities cross the gender lines for an even more interesting blend of people. Think of it as God's little way to mix and match!

Even Our Culture Has Personality

It's not just people who are created as opposite-but-complementary male and female; the world seems to be divided into two different but complementary halves as well.

- Western culture overall seems more Choleric, valuing production, invention, construction, and conquering. We're also the loud Sanguine rabble-rousers who know how to have fun while getting into plenty of trouble at the same time!

- Eastern culture overall appears to be more Phlegmatic, valuing quiet, calm, contemplation, and meditation. They work hard but quietly, getting overly dramatic about very little. The East is also Melancholy, practicing perfect respect, honor, and graciousness, even in the little things.

You have to be careful about this type of overgeneralizing, though, because every country and culture includes people of all four personalities. Your national heritage does not determine your natural temperament. However, it's fun to note how some countries and their customs seem to have taken on a personality of their own:

- Mexican siestas are definitely Phlegmatic! Enough work, let's take a nap.
- Proper British high tea is an elegant Melancholy event, done perfectly.
- Asian technical advances manifest as genius Melancholy.
- Irish rovers are often considered to be Sanguine storytellers.
- Germans are often hardworking Cholerics who dislike non-productive people.

Of course, there is a little bit of all four personalities in every family, every community, and every continent. Wherever you have people, you will also have personalities!

Some Are Optimists and Some Are Pessimists

I thought I'd mix it up a little and try to get Hans, the networking marketing husband, out of his shell, so I asked him, "Hans, in life do you tend to see the glass as half full or half empty?"

Before he could open his mouth, Darlene answered for him: "Half empty." Hans ignored her and repeated to me as if his wife were not even there, "Half empty. And it's a good thing."

The other Melancholies in the room chuckled. I smiled and nodded in agreement.

"Yes, we optimists need you for balance!"

I reminded everyone that Sanguines are the most naturally optimistic, perhaps naively so, but so are Cholerics (who think they can always tackle any problem and win), as well as the good-natured, easygoing Phlegmatics, who go to great lengths to avoid seeing any trouble. But the more pessimistic Melancholy is doomed to see everything that could ever go wrong, to remember every past mistake, and to project misery into the future. But don't despair! When the competitor is about to beat us or the company is about to go under, we need the Melancholies to caution the rest of us (who may have our heads in the sand) and help us put it all back together again perfectly.

Everyone Needs to Feel in Control

Some people point to the personality charts and say, "See? That's me. Choleric. 'Basic need is to have control.' I like to be in control." But the reality is that *everyone likes to be in control*; it's human nature. It's part of our natural desire to protect ourselves.

The four personalities exercise control in different ways, according to their natural temperament.

- Some *take charge* (active) to be in control. (Do this!)
- Others *run away* (passive) or procrastinate to stay in control. (You can't make me!)

If you hear someone say, "That person is so controlling!" she can be talking about any of the personalities.

Your Strengths Can Become Weaknesses

Once I was in an audience when Florence was speaking and I heard her say, "No one here has any weaknesses." I remember perking up. "Your weaknesses are simply your strengths carried to extreme."

I liked that! I have no weaknesses! Now I tell everyone I know who is interested in learning the personalities that they have no weaknesses. They like that too. If only we could remember that those in our workplace—even those who grind on our last nerve—also have a genuine strength behind what we are seeing. They have

How the Personalities Control

Popular Sanguine *Need:* to feel loved and that all is well	Powerful Choleric *Need:* to feel effective and productive
Typical Control Responses making light of things laughing disarming being charming or flirtatious offering prizes being friendly with others minimizing the problem throwing a party	*Typical Control Responses* convincing presenting logic setting goals delegating asking clearly for what they need making quick decisions working hard trying to take over
Extreme Control Responses begging and pleading pouting tantrums hitting slapping whining crying appearing helpless pretending high drama seduction lies cheating and stealing	*Extreme Control Responses* manipulation glowering demanding hot temper yelling and screaming barking orders pushing and pulling hitting grabbing name calling cussing threatening with action punishment or penalties
Peaceful Phlegmatic *Need:* to keep the peace	Perfect Melancholy *Need:* to feel life is moving toward perfection
Typical Control Responses staying reasonably detached avoiding high drama doing exactly what they are told seeing what others need and doing it not thinking too deeply avoiding problems finding easy ways to do things being friendly on the surface	*Typical Control Response* keeping things organized creating and following plans researching all the details staying within the budget bringing meaning and beauty to their environment striving for perfection sacrificing selflessly
Extreme Control Responses nondisclosure quiet refusal procrastination hiding or running away avoiding and withdrawing the silent treatment secrets and lies giving only the minimum required answering, "Fine," "Nothing," "I don't care," or "Whatever," to every question	*Extreme Control Responses* threats of moodiness deep, dramatic sighs high drama well-planned silent treatment physically withdrawing nondisclosure withholding secrets and lies showing visible disappointment snide remarks quiet revenge

just let their selfishness or their emotions get in the way. *That's* the real problem, not the personality.

Sanguines love to tell colorful stories, but when their storytelling is fostered by an immature need for attention, they go on and on—never listening or allowing anyone else to get a word in edgewise. Their storytelling strength becomes a miserable weakness. They will end up losing the very thing they crave: people's love and acceptance.

Cholerics have a clear, logical way of seeing the world and usually know exactly what needs to be done. But when they try to tell everyone else what to do, and never open up to receive suggestions, they alienate others and lose the very thing they need: a loyal following.

Melancholies are driven to perfection in the things they love to do, and most of us enjoy the fruit of their creative labor. But when they demand unrealistically high standards from themselves or others—in areas that don't require perfection—they lose what they desire: people who understand them and really care.

Phlegmatics are adaptable and naturally able to go with the flow, which makes them easy to be around. No high drama! But when they never stand up for things that require courage or hard work, or face a situation that might create conflict, they lose the very thing they want: respect from others.

The natural virtues that come with each temperament are numerous, but each of the four personalities has a special gift for something required of *every* successful leader, employee, or co-worker. If you could become the perfect person in your workplace, you would have the strengths of all four temperaments and the weaknesses of none. "Hmm . . . does such a person exist?" I asked the class. "In a person's own mind, probably. In reality, there are few. But is such a lofty goal worth working toward?"

"Yes!" called out—guess who?—Howard. He was excited and his enthusiasm was becoming contagious. "I love this stuff. It's fun!" he added.

"Right on target, Howard. Let's talk about fun."

Everyone Likes to Have Fun

In our seminars, we see people focus too much on a single personality attribute instead of the bigger picture. "Oh! 'Prone to depression'—*you* must be Melancholy!" But since everyone can be depressed at some time in their life, this may only cause us to identify ourselves—or someone we know—as a personality they are not.

"One lady had come up to me at an event and said, 'I like to have fun, so I must be Sanguine,'" I said. "Actually she was a Phlegmatic dragged to the event by her friend. She picked 'likes fun' so she could just be Sanguine and get it over with. It was easier than taking the test."

Remember that *everyone likes to have fun*. Some have fun in groups; some like solitary fun. Fun can mean something different to each of the personalities.

Once I was in upstate New York with an associate, Michael, with whom I was producing a DVD series. He's the creative-genius type and an award-winning director of television commercials. He's so Melancholy that he wears his favorite color—black—from head to toe every day.

Once after a taping session, we headed out to lunch through a dark, snow-covered landscape in the dead of winter. The trees were bare, like skeletons sticking out of the frozen ground. Despite my many-layered clothes, I was still shivering, and the darkening skies made me tired and depressed.

The dismal skies made Michael happy; he couldn't wait to introduce me to his favorite East-Coast restaurant chain that served large, cafeteria-style buffet meals. He liked to be able to study every dish; analyze the color, smell, and appearance of the entrees; and control the portions on his plate. As we drove toward the restaurant, the gloomy chill that was a heavy weight on me was a lovely melancholy backdrop to Melancholy Michael.

I'm the opposite—Sanguine. I live in the sunny Southern California desert where it is always warm and shining, and my idea of a nice lunch is being outdoors on the patio where someone is serving me a healthy salad sprinkled with goat cheese, toasted almonds, and dried cherries. Lunch in a stuffy old hotel where I have to serve myself, grab a plastic tray, and choose from Wonder bread, watery pasta, and cold apple pie didn't seem very exciting to me. But the restaurant had history (Melancholies love history), and the old-fashioned food brought back memories of Michael's childhood. I was miserable; he was happy. He looked out at the wintery doom and gloom swirling around us and said, "Isn't this *fun?*"

"So remember," I said, "each of the personalities has an idea of 'fun,' and that doesn't make them all Sanguine. Don't think you can be like Michael at the cafeteria, going down the line of personalities, picking and choosing the traits *you* want (or that you want others to have) and rejecting the rest."

"Cherry-picking personalities wouldn't be a very accurate application of your personality theory, would it?"

"No, Dr. Hastings, it wouldn't," I replied.

I walked over to him with a smile, stood next to his chair, and addressed the group. "Dr. Hastings is the perfect Melancholy who is all about accuracy and perfection. Let's be thankful for that and hope that none of us here ever has to go under the knife with a— God forbid!—*Sanguine surgeon!*"

Everyone laughed and Dr. Hastings smiled proudly.

As the group gathered up their books and left the room, I added, "Come back next time and we'll talk about perfect personality pairs! *And I'm not talking shoes!*"

What Did We Learn This Time?

- Don't be too quick to assess someone's personality—give it time.
- People can be introverts, extroverts, or a combination of both.
- You can learn new behavior, but your natural personality is your default mode.
- Everyone likes to control, but they do it in different ways.
- Strengths carried to extremes become weaknesses.

5

Personalities in Pairs

Choleric-Sanguine Howard Jones, the restaurateur, had gotten his second cup of coffee and stuck a chocolate donut in his mouth and was still chewing when he walked up and made a comment to us before class began.

"Hey, Rose. You and Florence keep telling us that you're both Choleric and Sanguine, but I'm starting to see some differences. *I think you're more Sanguine than Florence.*"

"Well . . . you got me, Howie!" I (Rose) said. "But as a Sanguine yourself you probably have an uncanny knack for spotting others who are just like you. Right?" He beamed. Sanguines are suckers for a compliment any day, any time.

"Yes, Rose is a bit more Sanguine," Florence told Howard. Then she turned to me. "Go ahead. Tell them how you forgot the paper." I laughed and shared one of our recent writing experiences.

"It's true. While I function mostly in my Choleric mode at work, overall I'm a little more Sanguine than Florence. While she and I were writing this book, I planned to go to her home where we'd spend the day together going over the chapters. I went early to my office, grabbed the manuscript, my snacks, my cell phone, charger, several pens, two red Flair markers, and a folder that holds paper, business cards, and has a built-in calculator."

Florence hugged me when I arrived, and we promptly sat down in her living room to get to work. We both took out our copies of the manuscript and our pens and began to make corrections. Florence likes to write longhand and soon asked me if I had any extra paper. She'd just returned after a speaking tour and was out of tablets. I looked in my folder. Uh-oh. I had only three sheets left of my yellow-lined paper, which I offered her. I felt like the little boy who gave his loaves and fishes to Jesus. I hoped for a miracle.

"That's it?" Florence asked. Cholerics have a way of getting to the point that bypasses the niceties. I felt stupid. But then I laughed and made a joke out of it.

"Great. Here we are, both writers and we have no paper!" I looked over, counted her three pens, and smiled brightly. "*But we have pens!*"

Florence couldn't resist. She laughed, grabbed my folder, and pointed out to me that there was no paper in it, no business cards in the business-card slots, and probably the calculator didn't work. She also made fun of the old foam rubber lining that was sticking out the cracked plastic seams. Sanguines can try to be organized—and can make good progress through life—but they will always be Sanguine! Thank goodness Florence is Sanguine, too, but her Choleric side is always ready to take charge. For our lunch she'd planned ahead and bought some ground sirloin, and shortly after noon she assigned me to fire up the stovetop grill and cook our burgers. Before I made the patties, I removed my four rings, put them on the kitchen counter, and completely forgot about them until I was home later that night in bed. One was my newly received engagement ring, but my Melancholy fiancé—who would be aghast that I had been so careless with the expensive symbol of his love for me—will never know unless someday he reads this book.

77

Everyone Has a Natural Combination of Personalities

Even if you identify your primary temperament, you also have a secondary one that might not be so obvious. No person is only one personality, because the four are really two sets of opposites—how you see life (perception) and how you move through it (pace). Everyone has one of each. Everyone is born with a "perfect pair" that's just right for them.

Sanguine and Melancholy—OPPOSITES—
You can only pick one!

These two "default" modes determine *how you see life*: optimistic, light, and carefree (Sanguine), or more naturally wary, concerned, and deep (Melancholy). Away from work, which one suits you most of the time in most circumstances?

> *Sanguines*—They are bouncing balls of high energy that tend to stay on the surface where things are open to the light, where they can keep things easy and fun. Sometimes they lose ground and drift up into the air (hence the often terrible but realistic name *airheads*). *Often Sanguines have no boundaries*, lose their belongings, and invade others' workspaces. They'll buy you a plant for your desk without ever asking if you have allergies! They want to touch and be touched, and their tendency will be to walk right up and give you a long embrace. Melancholies who see them coming will want to run!

> *Melancholies*—They are intense but low-key, burrowing deeply into the realities of life, not afraid of the dark and even preferring to go into the mysteries of it. They are grounded in reality and know that details do matter, especially when others fail to see their importance. They are good at discerning and making important, critical observations about things. They are warm and loving once you have earned their trust, but

Melancholies tend to protect their space by keeping a safe distance physically and emotionally.

Choleric and Phlegmatic—OPPOSITES— You can only pick one!

These two "default" modes determine *how you move through life*: quick and furious (Choleric) or calm and steady (Phlegmatic). Which one are you most like—away from work—when you are in your most natural state?

Cholerics—They go through life quickly, with fiery energy; their focus is out in the distance, on the end goal. They take charge quickly—without being asked—but often step on others' toes. Loud and intense, they can offend the more sensitive types. Cholerics race through the day, maintain a high speed through the evening, and then crash at the end. They race for the prize, tend to focus on the destination, and in their hurry often miss the beauty of the process.

Phlegmatics—They are more careful, steady, and able to focus more immediately on what is around them. They can maintain a steady speed, and they are smart enough to rev up only when absolutely necessary. When pushed, though, or rushing to get home to the couch, they will work as hard as a Choleric. They don't worry too much about the end result, being much more focused on the people and the process. They calm others down and make excellent mediators.

I finished and we were a little surprised when schoolteacher Carmen spoke up again. At first she'd been quiet, but now she seemed to really be opening up to this group.

"Florence, Rose—I'm *really* understanding this! I knew right away that I was Melancholy, but I also see another natural side of me. In my classroom I function as the in-charge Choleric—because

I have to. But from what I've been learning I think I'm mostly Melancholy with a secondary Phlegmatic side. I love peace and quiet!" She laughed sweetly at herself.

She was very gentle, and we could see everyone was happy to hear from her. Howard had found a permanent seat next to her in the last few sessions. They had both introduced themselves as single. Would they hit it off?

Now that she'd spoken up, Carmen kept talking. "I am such a stickler for detail and analysis, and I want the students to learn to do things well. But they wear me out. I can hold my own because I really love what I do—and the kids—but all I want to do at night is head for the sofa. And I hate when there is chaos in the classroom. So my combination makes me a Perfect Peaceful . . . right?"

Natural Combinations

The *Sanguine-Choleric* (double extrovert) combination says, "We'll all have fun as long as you do it my way!" They might not have the most class, but they brighten and lighten everyone's load. They do well as club or business presidents, as long as they function in their strengths. They love to be the up-front chairman, with opportunities to talk and boss people around. Think Bill Clinton.

The *Choleric-Melancholy* (extrovert-introvert) combination says, "I'll be in charge, and you'd all better do it perfectly!" This person may seem the most demanding, but she'll take the whole team to the finish line. Often people with this combination become the CEO and impress others with their flashes of brilliance. Think Hillary Clinton.

The *Melancholy-Phlegmatic* (double introvert) combination says, "I will sail the seven seas seeking perfection, but not if it makes any waves." You may have to work hard to earn this person's trust, but when she accepts you, she'll go to the ends of the earth for you. These are serious, thoughtful people who like to mediate problems or broker peace talks. Think Jimmy Carter.

The *Phlegmatic-Sanguine* (introvert-extrovert) combination says, "I really do like you just the way you are, and I only want to have fun!" These people are not the most productive, but they can be the most lovable. They see humor in everything, enjoy a good nap, avoid problems, and have no enemies. Think Ronald Reagan.

Florence went over and gave her a big hug. "Honey, *you're adorable!* And yes, you are a Perfect Peaceful!" As she was hugging Carmen, I saw her look over Carmen's shoulder and give Howard a little wink.

Then Florence pointed to the chart I had brought to the front of the room and asked, "Here are the natural personality combinations. Have you figured out what you are yet?"

You Can Develop All Strengths

I grew up trying to be a Melancholy, so I like to tell about what we call "masking" and didn't mind at all when Florence asked me to explain how some people lose touch with their natural personality.

"If you were born as a take-charge person, it will not come naturally for you to sit quietly with folded hands at the back of the room. With time and practice you can develop this habit but it is not your natural gift. And if you're a natural pessimist who sees the dark clouds even on sunny days, you can develop balance by seeing the bright side of life but you will never be a natural optimist."

Your realistic aim is to function in your strengths and work to overcome your weaknesses.

Being aware of the strengths of all four personalities and working hard to acquire the strengths that don't come naturally to you is a desired goal. But even when you adopt others' characteristics, you have not really changed your natural personality; you have simply matured into a well-balanced person. Your natural default will still dominate when there is no time to think or plan your reactions. Your realistic aim is to function in your strengths and work to overcome your weaknesses.

Sometimes We Wear a Mask

"However, sometimes we get confused and wear a personality mask so others will accept us," I continued.

81

My father brought me into his commercial real estate appraisal business in 1979, where I became an expert in real estate valuation. Sometimes I love to wear bright colors with big earrings and matching polka-dot eyeglasses, but I've often been called into superior court to testify as an expert in court cases. My attorney advised me, "Rose, you need to wear navy blue with a white blouse. Navy connotes authority. You have authority, but you need to look like you do. Small earrings. Low heels. And get some plain glasses, please."

I wasn't offended. I knew that the minute I stepped into the witness box the jury would take one look at this Sanguine and think, *How can she know anything?* For the sake of getting people to believe my testimony, I had to wear a Melancholy "mask."

Holly Homes piped up: "Rose! Me, too! When I told my agent I wanted to start selling more high-end properties, she told me I would have to change my whole wardrobe. Less flashy and more refined. I knew she was right."

"Thanks, Holly. That's exactly what I'm talking about. But tell the group what you wear on your days off."

Holly laughed. "I wear my funky outfits and flashy jewelry. I can't help it! I'm still Sanguine through and through!"

It's possible—and sometimes necessary—to modify your behavior without really changing your God-given personality. But sometimes we behave the way someone else tells us to because we are afraid. Because of abuse or other outside forces, some people lose sight of their true personality and wear a "mask" of another personality so others don't reject them. Parents, teachers, spouses, employers—and even our culture—can make us feel that if we are not who they want us to be, we are worthless. So we put on that mask, trying to be someone else, and can find ourselves exhausted or depressed by the end of the day.

One of the most common forms of "masking" is men who are afraid to be labeled as a peaceful Phlegmatic because they *want* to be a powerful Choleric. They don't realize that each personality has its own way to be "powerful," and it's often the stubborn Phlegmatic with the steady will of iron who really wins, while the frustrated Choleric huffs and puffs, then finally walks away. If we wrongly label Phlegmatics as lazy, or Melancholy as too depressing, no one will want to be either one of those.

Every time I hear Florence speak, I watch people naturally fall in love with her and her commanding-yet-sparkling Choleric-Sanguine personality. In fact, after they take the Personality Profile, I'm always amazed at how 99 percent of the audience scores as Choleric or Sanguine! They admire Florence and want to be like her. But most of them are not seeing the wonderful gifts of their true personality.

Our Body Speaks a Paired Personality Language

"What people wear, how they walk, talk, sit, and stand can give clues to their personality," I said.

"Yeah, Holly! The Bauble Queen!" Howard hollered out. Even though everyone knew Howard was attracted to Carmen, he loved to banter with Holly. Sanguines just love other Sanguines.

Physical postures and tones of voice speak the language of the personalities without words. Florence is famous for her saying, "A Phlegmatic would rather lean than stand, rather sit than lean, and rather lie down than sit." Audiences always laugh, because it's funny and true a lot of the time, but not always.

PHLEGMATIC COMBINATIONS

Phlegmatics as a whole do tend to walk slower, and you can see the ultra-relaxed attitude in their stance. They *do* lean! They tend to have a steady and purposeful gait and a quiet voice. Most of the time they will wear neutral colors that prevent them from standing out (unless they are also part artistic Melancholy or flashy Sanguine). They are also very adaptable—one of their great strengths—and will pick up on the traits of those around them to fit in. I know one Phlegmatic man who walks as though he is in a constant footrace, speeding here and there frenetically. He appears Choleric but he's not. He feels the pressure of what he has to get done and he hopes that, if he moves faster, he will be able to go home and plop into his easy chair sooner.

- The *Phlegmatic-Sanguine*, when feeling emotionally safe and comfortable, will often move into the Sanguine side with a louder voice, funny stories, and more colorful clothes. But they will still be hesitant and careful when necessary and will not want to offend anyone.
- The *Phlegmatic-Melancholy*, in an artistic mode, may wear bright colors, too, but will still be more reserved than the Sanguine. However, the starched, precise Melancholy will insure that this combination never draws too much attention to oneself. Keep the peace. Don't offend.

CHOLERIC COMBINATIONS

Cholerics tend to be louder and more intense when speaking with others. Some people think they are always yelling when they are not. At least *they* don't think so. They are fast with words and retorts and are quick to laugh, sometimes *at* others rather than *with* them. "Often they use big physical gestures when expressing themselves," I said. "Like the other extroverts, Sanguines, they often like to call attention to themselves in what they wear as if to say, 'See me? I am in charge here. Don't you forget it.'"

Everyone heard soft-spoken Hans mutter quietly, "Don't worry, I'll *never* forget it!"

I continued:

- The *Choleric-Sanguine* almost always feels free to speak with a loud voice, walk quickly, touch others, invade space, be restless, and literally look around for the next task or fun event.

84

They have animated faces and voices and like costumes and funny hats.

- The *Choleric-Melancholy* may wear bright colors and accessories (ties for men), too, but they are fashionably refined and will never want to look as foolish as the Sanguine combination might. When they are worried or hurt, they will move into their Melancholy mode and be more reserved with their body language, voice, and facial expressions.

One of my real estate friends, Lisa, has used personalities in her office for years. She told us the story of a loud person at her workplace. "I called her privately into my office and told her she was too loud and that some of the customers and co-workers had complained. But instead of just putting her down, I gave her some practical steps to help her improve, and she did!"

Remember that many of these outward signs are often developed as a result of company dress codes, age, social background, and peer pressure, and may not always reveal a person's true temperament. Don't make the mistake of identifying someone's personality based on only a few visible signs or over a short period of time.

Lisa's Five Steps

Before you open your mouth:
1. Think
2. Edit
3. Soften
4. Edit again
5. Speak!

Perfect Pairs Can Also Rub the Wrong Way

The opposite personalities are meant to be a good balance to each other. In marriage, opposites often attract to bring something to the relationship that the other doesn't naturally have.

In the workplace, a "marriage" of opposite Cholerics and Phlegmatics—or Sanguines and Melancholies—can make the perfect pair for the job, the team, or the company.

But opposites can also rub the wrong way.

As we write this book, our country is in an economic recession that's been so devastating that it's been named the Great Recession. There's not a business that is unaffected, and this slump can cause negative emotions. This is when we slip easily into our weaknesses:

The Sanguine, unable to concentrate.

The Choleric, impatient and angry.

The Melancholy, moody and depressed.

The Phlegmatic, remote and fearful.

I told the group that this had happened to me recently, with my Melancholy-Phlegmatic office manager—the perfect pair for my Sanguine-Choleric nature: she remembered when I forgot and cleaned up when I made a mess. We'd worked together for three years and I depended on her to keep things running smoothly. As I've always done, I paid her on an above-average basis with lots of perks and freedom to come and go as she needed. As happens with co-workers, we shared our personal and family ups and downs, and we'd been a support to each other outside the office. We were friends. We were a perfect pair.

Unfortunately, income had been drastically low for several months, and I knew I had to tell her that I'd either have to let her go or cut her pay until things improved, which I was sure would happen eventually. We'd been in these tight spots before. At first, I introduced this sensitive topic rather matter-of-factly. "Renee, we need to talk about money. You've seen the income dwindling these last few months. We might have to start really cutting back immediately. I need to know how much you'd be willing and able to reduce your pay, temporarily of course, until things pick up. Can you talk to your husband about it and get back with me tomorrow?" I knew I had to give her time and space to think about it.

Renee is a balanced Phlegmatic, so she listened patiently, made no comments, and agreed to get back to me. The next day our discussion took a different turn. She and her husband were facing economic fears, and I, too, was worried about my financial future. Our emotions were high. She told me she thought I was being insensitive to her personal economic situation.

Me? Insensitive? The perfect boss? My voice rose ten decibels, straining my throat and making my heart pound. Then I began to recount all the years I'd carried the business alone, all the people I'd hired and overpaid, all the people I'd helped, and all the people who had failed me in the last twenty years—as though any one of them had anything to do with Renee! She tried to say something, but I held up my hand and cut her off. "I'm sorry; right now I'm too emotional. I need to calm down. We need to talk about this later." She said nothing. As a Phlegmatic she usually waits for others to lead the situation.

About a half hour later I went into the bathroom, looked in the mirror, and made a sad face at myself. I prayed, "Oh, God, I *am* sorry for letting my emotions take over. I need to trust you more and worry less. We will get through this. I know it. I just don't feel it right now."

I knew I needed to go right back out and tell Renee I was sorry for my outburst and to tell her that no matter what she needed to do, I would respect it and we would work through this tough time together. So I did. I walked up close to her desk, hung my head in a humble but humorous way, and began to apologize. ". . . and I know in the big scheme of things, Renee, we'll be okay. I'll do whatever is necessary to get us both through this. Will you forgive me?"

"There's nothing to forgive," she said politely. "But I appreciate what you're saying," and she turned back to her computer.

Now, after conflict resolution, what does a Sanguine want to do immediately? *Hug.* It's the physical affirmation of the verbal agreement. It is the act that seals the deal. I just wanted us to be happy again and enjoy the rest of the day. Now in some workplaces a hug might not be appropriate, but Renee and I were close. Is one little hug too much to ask for two people who had worked together, side by side, for years?

But I remembered that Renee is a sensitive Melancholy who likes her space, and a Phlegmatic who doesn't want to be forced or pushed into anything (without due consideration and full consent of her will), so I took a deep breath, turned, and walked back to my desk. No hugs today.

It's okay, I said to myself. I was satisfied knowing I had respected her personality to the point of sacrifice. I gave up my need for the hug and instead gave her what *she* needed: space.

Renee had also been learning about personalities. Later, after lunch, she said, "Rose, you know when you came out of the bathroom and walked right up to my chair and said you were sorry?"

"Yeah?"

"Well, I was acutely aware of being Melancholy-Phlegmatic. When I saw you coming and heard you saying you were sorry, with your shoulders down, I thought, *Uh-oh, she is going to want a hug. What will I do?* I froze up for an instant and made a plan while you talked. *I know! If she moves toward me with her arms out, I will hug her. But if she doesn't, I won't.* And you didn't. So I didn't. Isn't that funny?"

I didn't see what was so humorous. If I wasn't going to get the hug, now I wanted credit for my sacrifice. "See, Renee? I *knew* you didn't want to hug me and I was being sensitive to you! See?"

She was smiling but she didn't say anything. She wasn't even going to give me credit, either! *Arghh-h-h!* I gave up and went back to my desk. Work always makes me feel better anyway.

"Showing affection comes naturally to some, to others it may even feel inappropriate," I reminded the class. "Some just need a little time and space. Some need a friendly touch. Let's be willing to give others what they need."

We saw heads nodding at that last remark.

"Thank you, Rose," Florence said. "Even though Rose and I are similar in our personalities, I *am* more Choleric than she is. In fact, my personality has opened the door for me for many years in quite a few leadership positions. Especially when I was president."

President? Puzzled looks were on people's faces. Florence has a natural flair for the dramatic and in fact was a favorite high school drama teacher before she married Fred. So I felt it my duty to rescue the students from their confusion.

"Yes. There isn't a church ministry, community organization, PTA, or women's club that Florence ever joined where she didn't quickly rise to become . . . president! But lately I think she has set her sights even higher; she makes me call her Your Royal Highness now!"

Lots of laughter. The Sanguines loved the humor, but Melancholy Dr. Hastings raised his hand.

"I dare say that I speak for us all," he nodded politely to the others in the room, "that you two have given us a very thorough overview of the four personalities, their strengths and weaknesses, and the natural combinations. But is there a chart, graph, or quick-reference list that we can use to work with them?"

(Leave it to a Melancholy to get the Sanguines back on track!) Florence nodded to me that she would take over from here.

"Yes, Dr. Hastings," Florence said. "Our next four classes will focus more intently on each of the four personalities in the workplace, and we'll give you charts and quick-tip lists that we think you'll find extremely helpful."

And with that, she couldn't resist regally raising her hand and announcing, "Class dismissed." Holly Homes and Fran Taylor giggled, grabbed their notebooks, stood up, and curtsied before leaving the room together.

What Did We Learn This Time?

- Everyone has a primary and secondary personality.
- These personalities may be balanced, or one may be more dominant.
- Sometimes people wear a "mask" to get along or be accepted.
- *Sanguines* and *Melancholies* are opposites—you can be one or the other, not both.
- *Cholerics* and *Phlegmatics* are opposites—you can be one or the other, not both.
- Choleric-Sanguine combinations work hard and make things fun.
- Choleric-Melancholy combinations work hard and expect perfection.
- Phlegmatic-Sanguine combinations are balanced and make things fun.
- Phlegmatic-Melancholy combinations are purposeful and balanced.

PART 2

WORKING
WITH THE
PERSONALITIES

6

Popular Personality

Sanguine

"Are we going to start with the Sanguines?" Howard asked loudly as he entered our classroom. Carmen, right beside him, shushed him quietly and tried to tone him down.

"Yes, Howard," I (Florence) replied. "This is the most fun of all."

"See, Carmen? You will learn to appreciate me."

She sat down without another word, and he put his arm around her in a protective manner.

Holly bounced in, wearing new white shoes.

"Look what I got—new shoes. They have springs in them somewhere and they are guaranteed to make you have a spring in your step."

Howard took a long look at Holly's feet and added, "I like springs. Do they work?"

Holly jumped up and down and showed us all how the springs worked.

As she was bouncing, Fran entered and seemed to get a little excited.

"Hey, Fran, you wanna try on my new shoes?"

Rose could see that we were losing any sense of order. "Okay, everyone," she said. "Let's applaud Holly's performance and get down to work."

Holly quietly handed the springy shoes to Fran, who left them on the floor, sensing this was not the time to put on another demonstration.

I moved up, smiling at the girls, and began our lesson.

"What we have just seen is an example of our reactive personalities. Sanguine Howard came in talking loudly, and Sanguine Holly bounced in wearing her own set of trampolines. This drew attention to Holly."

Fran spoke up. "I'm half Sanguine, and I jumped right in, wanting to try them on. I still do, but I'm trying to be polite instead."

We all agreeed that Fran's restraint was commendable, and she handed the shoes back to Holly.

"Later," she said, with a smile.

"Our lesson today is on the Sanguines," I began. "So, it's appropriate that you Sanguines all started the class by drawing attention to yourselves. This is one of the key personality traits, innately wanting to be the center of all attention and doing things that keep people's eyes on you. On the positive side, this is excellent in leadership and motivating others. You know how to get attention, but can you keep it, and if so, do you have anything new—and instructive—to say?"

As we look at the Sanguine strengths, we must remember that strengths carried to extremes become weaknesses. It's great that Sanguines can converse with anyone quickly. This trait is exceptional, but carrying it too far leads to babbling on when others wish you'd stop.

Fred and I were taking a couple out to Sunday brunch when a Sanguine friend from Australia, John, arrived a day early to visit us. We explained we had plans but that he could join us. When we sat down to eat, John began to talk and talk and talk. Melancholy Fred timed him, and after thirty-eight minutes Fred interrupted and thanked John for his stories but moved the conversation on to Floyd and Pat, our invited guests. Floyd, a Melancholy dental surgeon, began sharing about an experience he'd had that reminded John of another event. With his mouth full of mashed potatoes, he jumped right in, totally unaware he was usurping the attention—again.

The next morning at breakfast, after Fred had left the table, John leaned over and quietly said, "I was so embarrassed when Fred interrupted me in front of those people yesterday."

I countered with, "John, do you know how long you talked before Fred interrupted?"

"Just a few minutes, not very long."

"John, you talked without a breath for thirty-eight minutes."

"No, I didn't!"

"Yes, you did. Fred timed you."

What could John say?

"Our lesson for you Sanguines is that a little of your chatter goes a long way," I told the class. "Fred helped me learn discipline by suggesting that when two or three stories come to my mind, I should choose only one. Even though they all are brilliant."

"Am I like that?" Howard asked.

Carmen's big brown eyes got bigger, but she didn't answer, even though the others nodded toward Howard.

"Wow!" he blurted out, "I guess I'll have to watch out for that." Howard was unusually quiet for the rest of our session.

Fran spoke up and asked, "Could I tell a story about how my husband and I handled our personality differences?"

I didn't need another example, but Fran had been relatively quiet for a Choleric-Sanguine and I felt I owed her some time in our small spotlight.

Darlene called out, "I didn't know you were married."

"Well, I am, but he's Phlegmatic and doesn't like to come to things like this. But I don't mind because we've worked our business out so we divide our responsibilities. Besides my fashion business we own a video production company that films fashion shows. Working together in the business with my husband is such fun. Even though we didn't know or understand the personalities, we somehow did it right. I love the marketing and networking part of our business since it's so people focused. I find time to go to many events and industry meetings, and I make lots of contacts and new friends. My Phlegmatic husband is just the opposite. He really enjoys staying in the comfort of our home office, keeping all the records and planning our schedules.

Sanguines tend to be forgetful.

"The last time we went together to a company event, he walked into the room with me, made friends with one person, and stayed there all evening. I, on the other hand, made sure I went to every table and met every single person face-to-face. When we got home that night, I dumped my purse out on the bed. I'd collected more than thirty business cards!

"There are lots of other perks from being able to network like that," Fran concluded. "By taking the time and having the energy to meet everyone, not only did I make all those business contacts, I also ended up with two free tickets to a revival of *Oklahoma*!"

We all cheered and started to sing, "Oh, What a Beautiful Morning." But as much fun as we were having, I needed to get them back together one more time.

"Let me tell you, I think you're all turning into a bunch of Sanguines," I said.

"You said we were going to have fun today" Dr. Hasting added, "And I'm really trying."

"Let's try listening for a few minutes," I said. "Then I want to let you laugh over me and my trouble with losing things—primarily my keys."

Losing the Keys

Sanguines frequently lose their keys. They need to use their hands for expressive communication, so they drop their car keys—or purse, or sunglasses—down wherever they are. They move on to find a new audience and by the day's end have no idea where they laid down their things. They might not even think about the keys until they go out to the car and can't get in. But even worse than that is how often we lose them even at home.

Fred helped me with this by hammering a nail into the wall near the door where I came in from the garage. He pointed out how easy it would be for me to always hang my big ring of keys there each time I entered. It made sense, but the problem was that I forgot to use his system. He then made extra sets of keys for me and scattered them around the house. This was a help for me and became a game for my children. "Mother has to go to the store," I'd announce. "Who can be the first to help me find a set of keys?"

Fred did his best to help me without saying, "Your mother is hopeless." After Fred died, I found a small chain of keys in his desk with a large plastic label that read, "Unknown keys from Flo's key ring," dated 10/96. I have no idea what they open, but Fred is still helping me from the grave!

Sanguine Characteristics

Sanguines tend to be forgetful. They are so busy telling stories, entertaining people, and engaging people in conversation that they may forget what they are supposed to be doing—which can, of course, cause problems for co-workers.

Spending

One other problem Sanguines have is with spending. With them it is a hobby. The Sanguines love to buy clothes, spend money, and become trendsetters. They think credit cards are gift cards and don't read the notices sent to show them that the interest rates on their charges have doubled. One Sanguine woman we spoke with about her financial problems admitted she had no idea what her credit card interest rate was. "I just pay whatever the minimum charge is each month and feel like I'm putting money in the bank." A debt-straddled Sanguine on the Suze Orman show confessed she owed forty-four thousand dollars in credit card bills. Should this strike a note of fear in your Sanguine heart, do as Suze recommended: "Learn to add, cut up your credit cards, and shop at Wal-Mart!"

"If you are *not* Sanguine, you may also have trouble with money," I said. "You Cholerics, Darlene and Fran, just don't have the time to count or worry about the credit card balance; you'll deal with *that* crisis when it comes later. However, a shocking interest rate increase may scare you into paying timely attention. You Cholerics are essential in the business world, but we must watch over you as we would a sneaky child as you tend to take big chances."

The Sanguines love to buy clothes, spend money, and become trendsetters.

I moved around the room. "And the Melancholies—like you, Carmen and Dr. Charles—love adding columns and creating budgets and rarely make mistakes. You two are obviously above average and probably never get yourself in trouble. But Melancholies do tend to get depressed at having to actually live on a budget. If a problem arises, they often blame it on the company. If the creditors come knocking on their door, they often point to their perfect system and wonder what went wrong."

As I turned to Hans and Pastor Paul, Hans said, "I don't pay any attention to the money. That's Darlene's area."

"That's good, Hans, but some Phlegmatics have to handle their money. They might wait with their head in the sand until the credit card crisis is so overwhelming that maybe someone else—like

Darlene—will finally take charge and rescue them from the problems they have created by procrastinating."

We could have continued, but it was time to get the class back on track. "One of my Sanguine problems is I love sales and I somehow feel that if you buy a $100 outfit for $50 you earned $50 so now you can spend more," I said.

"That's what I do, too," laughed Holly. "Some days I really save a lot by spending more!"

Pastor Paul spoke up. "One of the things I hate—I guess I should say dislike—about Sanguines is that they volunteer to do everything but they do nothing. I'm sure they mean well, but they don't follow through. I've learned in my church that you can't count on them. The worst thing is that if you don't give them a job, they get hurt and tell everyone you don't like them. We have one woman, Cathy—behind her back the other women call her Chatty Cathy—who talks too much, like that Australian fellow you told about. She volunteered to get my Thursday morning Bible study outline printed for me. When she didn't show up, I called her and she said, 'Oh, is it Thursday already?' The next week I phoned her on Wednesday to remind her. She got mad at me, and the next morning she was running late, there was a long line at Kinko's, they ran out of pink paper, and she walked in when we were almost finished. I thanked her and never asked her to do anything again. She never came again, and now she's changed churches."

Our little group groaned at the pastor's profile of a Sanguine, and I realized how they had grown to be supportive of one another and to look forward to our weekly gatherings. What we had planned to be a study had become a social club. Rose passed out the Sanguine charts for them to take home to study. When class dismissed, they all left the room together to go out for coffee, and Darlene called back to me, "Next time we'll talk about me, right?"

As I nodded, Hans smiled at me as if to say, *Good luck, honey.*

How to Work with a Sanguine: Quick Tips

Now that you've read their stories and know the signs of sunny Sanguines, what will you do if you work with a Sanguine? If you're the opposite, Melancholy, please don't give up yet! The following is a quick-reference list with helpful tips for getting along with and supporting a Sanguine customer, client, employee, leader, or co-worker. And if you're a Sanguine who's been put in a position of leadership in your workplace, we hope you can use this list to stay operating in your strengths instead of your weaknesses. If you do, everyone will have fun and be glad you come to work each day.

What Did We Learn This Time?

This time we have a helpful reference chart to help you with Sanguines!

How to Help Sanguines at Work
"They talk all the time and think everything is funny!"

Basic desire	Learn to:
Have fun	Appreciate their need for appropriate fun in the workplace
Emotional needs	
Approval	Be generous with authentic praise and compliments
Attention	Listen even when they ramble
Affection	Don't withhold; give appropriate smiles, hugs, winks, and pats
Fun	Let them have their fun and plan appropriate fun for others
Get depressed when	
Feeling unloved or overwhelmed by work	See them less for what they do and more for who they are; try a personal connection
Control by	
Charm and humor	Don't let them minimize issues; lovingly let them know you need their sensitivity

Best at	
Making initial contact with people	Put them on the phone or at the front desk
Creating enthusiasm and excitement	Ask what they think and then thank them
Encouraging and uplifting others	Don't put them down when they cheer others up
Ensuring the group has fun	Invite their ideas for injecting some fun into the assignment
Lightening a somber mood	Respect their optimism
Seeing the sunny side	Appreciate the balance they bring to problems
Being on stage	Help them keep to a time limit
Charming others to work	Put them in manager positions with strong Melancholy support
Remembering color and design	Help them with the details
Not holding grudges	Praise them for this
Volunteering for jobs	Thank them, ask what they need to get the job done right, and then remind them to do it
Thinking up new ways to do things	Don't put down an idea until you give it full consideration
Starting in a flashy way	Thank them for motivating others and helping them with follow-through
Looking great on the surface	Stand by them when they fail; assign others to the deeper areas
Speaking up quickly	Thank them for being good communicators
Giving warm and friendly greetings	Understand they're being genuine and appreciate it
Being colorful and demonstrative	Ask them to give explanations or share in boring meetings
Bringing fun to the workplace	Put them in charge of parties, luncheons, and holiday celebrations
Nurturing those who hurt	Give them the freedom to hug, reassure, and cheer others
Moving quickly past the problems	Affirm them to others as examples of letting go and moving on

Making friends easily	Ask them to break the ice and get people mixing
Being the life of the party/a storyteller	Encourage them at the right time
Bonding quickly but moving on	Don't take it personally when they forget you; they still love you

Presentation style

Have a light, humorous touch	Help them stay on track with the facts
Are cheerful and bubbling over	Stay open to their enthusiasm

Problems

Are easily distracted and have a poor memory	Set up a reminder system that works for them
Forget to follow through	Ask someone to be their "reminder coach"
Don't pay attention to details	Don't nag; pair them with a Melancholy
Don't always plan or prepare ahead	Help them with making charts and schedules
Can come on too happy or too cute	Explain the Melancholy mind to them
Aren't very goal-oriented	Help them write goals and save them in a computer file
Compulsive talker	Use a gentle touch to help them stop
Seem phony to some	Explain/defend their sincerity to others
Are loud/scare others off	Teach them about other personality needs; they'll love it
Attach to others indiscriminately	Help them with boundaries
Get depressed when work is no fun	Give frequent rewards/lunches
Hate to work alone	Make sure they have an office or assignment buddy
Need to be center stage	Create appropriate time and place for this
Interrupt and/or answer for the quiet ones	Thank them and, *with humor*, ask them to let the quiet ones talk
Make excuses	Use the Oreo approach: *reassure, correct,* and *thank* them

Their confidence fades fast	Send them to school, get them training, assign a helper
Bluster and complain	Sometimes just ignore it—they will get over it more quickly than most; if complaints persist, listen sympathetically
Look for credit	Praise them when it's deserved
Speak/act without thinking	Teach them a "fun" method of slowing down
Inappropriately hug or touch	Teach them to be careful about touching others and to respect physical boundaries
Have restless energy	Keep them busy
Exaggerate or even lie	Understand that they need attention; they may also need workplace counseling

Remember: Sanguines never let the facts stand in the way of a good story.

7

Powerful Personality

Choleric

When Rose and I (Florence) were ready to start our day of Choleric angst, Howard came rushing in, almost breathless.

"I think I just figured out my brother, Johnny. He told me his story last night and all of a sudden it came to me. He's Choleric and doesn't know it."

"How did you figure this out?" I asked.

"Well, he's thirty-three years old, can't seem to keep a job, thinks no one is as smart as he is, and can't adjust to the people at work. He calls them all idiots."

"And what have you decided?"

"See, Johnny likes outside sales, to be given a task, and sent out on his own to complete it. He's changed jobs so many times because each time the boss is wrong. Could every boss be as wrong as Johnny thinks they are?" Howard was starting to understand the Choleric weaknesses.

"I can tell from what he says that his current boss is probably an unhappy Melancholy. She's negative, pessimistic, and always mentions whatever went wrong and nothing that went right. Johnny thought he should point this attitude out to her so she could improve. Oh, brother! I bet that went over well!"

"How did she take that advice?" I asked.

"She was furious and told him she was the boss and didn't need his opinion. He said he was only trying to help. I guess some people just never want help."

"What happened then?" I asked.

"She fired him. I guess she just didn't want to improve, especially Johnny's way."

Choleric Characteristics

Cholerics want to help and often see what would work best. They are optimistic and tend to avoid emotions, even when it's normal or appropriate. They often dismiss others' fearful or worrisome feelings, priding themselves on their own tough constitution. But the perceived arrogance can shut everyone down. This may be the reason people like Johnny change jobs so frequently.

By knowing the strengths and weaknesses of the personalities, Johnny might be able to understand that some unmet emotional need is causing his Melancholy director to function in her weaknesses, but that she has strengths

> *Cholerics want to help. They are optimistic and tend to avoid emotions, even when it's normal or appropriate.*

he needs to appreciate. Maybe she would listen to him and even do what he suggests if he first listens to her. He could start with understanding and being sensitive to her in whatever way he can.

"I've been like that, too," Howard admitted. "My insensitivity to sensitive people has sometimes been a real problem. I guess

Cholerics need to slow down, shut their mouths, and just listen once in a while."

If you're Choleric, have you learned to listen and thank others for their opinion, even when you don't agree with them?

Like a Lion

Choleric-Sanguine Betsy knows that the personalities have their own "body language." Typically the two introverted personalities (Melancholy and Phlegmatic) keep their feelings and expressions under tight wraps, unless they are around those with whom they feel safe or familiar. When they feel emotionally safe, they can look and act like a natural extrovert. Not so for the extroverts (Sanguine and Choleric), whose natural tendency to display their feelings quickly is often misunderstood or can get them into trouble—like Betsy's Choleric "lion" side.

"When I'm under stress, I feel a powerful tightening that wells up in my chest and my angry/hungry Choleric wants to *leap out like a lion*! It's a signal to me that the problem is not others around me but my own natural response telling me either I haven't gotten enough rest or my Sanguine hasn't had enough fun," she said.

The workplace can be a jungle, and all the personalities will react differently to stressors. Often it will be seen in their physical responses. Cholerics are quick to anger. They begin to breathe rapidly; their movements may become quick and harsh, with clenched fists and/or pursed lips. Rose's sister, Malia, is a powerful Choleric who says that when the workplace gets stressful, she is "constantly gritting my teeth and stretching my lips into one thin line." When anything is out of control in a Choleric's life, he or she automatically starts to take it out on others.

Here are typical ways the other personalities respond to stress:

Sanguines—who by nature are sweet and childlike and want everyone to love them—can be quickly moved to tears by one big insult. Their typical reaction to such a stressful situation is to wander around from office to office, repeating their sad, hurtful tale, and looking for hugs and sympathy. They never seem to learn and their co-workers may think (or even say), "Grow up."

Melancholies—who are naturally sensitive—usually experience body weakness or stomach and bowel issues. One Melancholy man who was unhappy at his workplace got "food poisoning" almost every day, no matter where or what he ate. He complained of a weak or fluttering stomach and popped antacids as if they were gumdrops. Because he was holding his intense feelings inside, he was suffering physically.

Phlegmatics often suffer from physical exhaustion. One Phlegmatic in Rose's office was a hard worker but would get easily overwhelmed trying to keep up with the Cholerics. Every day about 4:00 p.m. he would disappear. She learned to look in the back room, where she could find him lying flat on the carpet, behind a desk, hands folded over his stomach, resting peacefully. The first time Rose walked in and found him lying on the floor, she thought he was dead. She cried out, "Joe! Are you sick?" and bent over to see if she could hear him breathing. Without moving a muscle or opening his eyes, he said quietly, "No, I'm just tired . . . and I need a nap."

Respect Is Key

I told the group about the workshops we often give. "Rose and I work together with our friend Tammy in what we call 'Upper Class.' The three of us spend several days working with small groups of those who want to be better public speakers. Judy is a Choleric who was one of our better students. When we told her we were teaching this class, she wanted to share what she thought would be good input for you all. Rose, why don't you read Judy's email?"

Rose read:

Success in business is impossible when people don't respect one another for their natural gifts. And let's face it: we're going to have to rub elbows with people who are completely different than we are. I believe that whether I'm speaking to one or a thousand, respect is key. And the best way to respect the audience is to know their personality needs.

Cholerics want to start and end a meeting on time. They want a clear takeaway that has value. Give them an outline or new brochure.

Sanguines need social contact that's fun. I've found no better way than to teach the personalities during staff meetings. It's about people . . . and it's fun!

Melancholies might at first be suspicious of your credibility, since they have high standards. They need to know your credentials right up front. Be kind and don't insult their intelligence.

Phlegmatics are worried about having to do too much work. Make materials simple and easy to read, with lots of fill-in-the-blanks to keep them alert. Encourage them to take down the details and give them blank pages for their notes.

Everybody wants respect, so teach them the personalities and help them enjoy each other's differences.

Impatient, or Something Else?

"Florence?" Carmen had raised her hand politely. "Those are good tips, but one of the things I struggle with the most is the impatience of the Choleric. How do we handle that?"

I thought about a story my friend Beverly had shared, and I told it to the class. "One Sunday at my friend Beverly's church, the sermon was given by a guest speaker. The man was raising money for returning veterans by selling bricks to some new building. Beverly was touched by his plea and after church went over to the table where the man was standing amid pictures and floor plans of the future facility."

When she handed him a one-hundred-dollar bill to buy two bricks, he pushed the money back and said, "Don't you have a credit card?"

She replied, "I want to give you the cash."

Impatiently he handed her a poorly printed page of charity information and brushed her off with: "If you really want to give cash, just mail it in to the address at the bottom of the page. They don't mind counting it."

As he turned to charm the next donor, Beverly decided she didn't need to give a donation badly enough to mail it.

"Sheesh! That guy really blew it," said Holly Homes.

"Yeah, that happens all the time in retail," said Fran Taylor. "On both sides of the counter. The impatient Choleric customer is not going to get the help of the salesclerk, who will go check on something and just not come back. And the crabby Choleric clerk will lose a sale—sometimes a big one—with that kind of impatience."

Rose reminded the class that even though the man in my story was an impatient Choleric, he could have been any one of the personalities.

A Sanguine may have been taught by the home office to run the credit card through the machine but not even thought to bring the cash box in from the car. Sanguines make their mistakes your problem.

A Melancholy may have spent a lot of time setting up the credit card system and believed it was the only right way for sales to be done—no other way.

A Phlegmatic may have wanted to do it the easiest way—for himself—and stubbornly refused to budge. Cash is "too much like work."

"I have something to say," said Pastor Paul. "I'm beginning to see these personality traits now everywhere I go. There's a verse in the Bible about scales falling from our eyes so that we can see truth more clearly. I don't mean to get too spiritual on everyone, but this class has really opened my eyes!" Everyone agreed.

Making Connections

After we took a short break and returned to our room, Dr. Hastings asked me if he could contribute to our discussion on Cholerics. "What Cholerics need to know," he said, "is that the rest of us sometimes need a safe emotional harbor."

"Emotional safety. Great choice of words, Doctor. Thank you," Hans said.

Dr. Hastings continued. "When I look back in my own family, I see now that my Choleric mother married a Phlegmatic and found herself wishing and hoping he'd change to be more like her. She gave him 'strong suggestions' that he seemed to ignore, and so she developed critical thoughts about a good man. In his deliberate, Phlegmatic style, wanting to avoid conflict and keep the peace, my father chose not to respond in an outwardly negative way about her complaints. I'm more like him."

"Wow, that's sad," said Fran. She didn't say more, but since Fran was Choleric I wondered if she was relating this story to her own life, knowing that there's more than likely an out-of-control Choleric somewhere in every family.

"Mother did eventually soften toward Dad, though," the doctor continued. "After we'd all moved out and had families of our own, Mother took another look at her own Choleric pushiness and her tendency to ignore my father's kind disposition. I'll never forget the day she admitted that Dad was able to handle conflict in a much nicer way, while she was the impatient nag."

Darlene spoke up. "I'm Choleric. I see myself in this. I hate to admit it but recently I've had my own moments of realizing how intrusive I've been with others. Not everyone likes me to barge into their office or ask about their personal lives. I used to think that because women can be more relational they should be comfortable coming and going into each other's physical or personal space. But they're not all that way. I've started backing off and giving others the time and space they need to respond."

Then she looked around at the group and leaned in a bit. "It's hard to be patient! It's not easy being Choleric!" The group laughed.

"Last week I hosted a wine and cheese gathering at my home for some of the people in our business. Hans helped me set up. As an activity I brought our class materials and we all took the personality test. Hoping we'd have some discussion about it, I purposely made it a small group where the introverts wouldn't feel overwhelmed and outnumbered. And sure enough, because it was an intimate and safe setting, many of them began to open up about the hardships in their lives. It was such a safe and supportive evening that no one wanted to go home!"

"Yes, dear. You gave them something better than wine and cheese," said Hans, and Darlene let him continue without interruption. "You gave them your time and undivided attention. And when you do that, I never want to leave either!"

"Rose?" Darlene asked. "Recently I read a *Time* magazine article in which the author surmised that people want satisfying marriages but don't want to work hard to get them. She said that we recognize marriage is something of great worth, but we are increasingly less willing to put in the hard work and sacrifices to get there.[3] It struck me—since Hans and I work together, too—that the same thing might be said of relationships at work. What do you think?"

"Yes, Darlene, you're right," Rose answered. "Some people want to get along with others in their company but don't want to put any effort into it. The cultural decline of happy marriages may also signal the decline of happy workplace relationships, which are our daytime 'marriages.' Do you realize that most people spend eight hours a day or more with the people at work and share more of their life with them than they do with their own spouse?"

"Like *Jon and Kate Plus Eight*," said Holly. "Those two worked together on that TV show about raising their eight children, and they ended up divorced."

"Yeah," added Hans a little bit defensively. "Because Kate was 110 percent Choleric. Her Phlegmatic husband, Jon, let her rule the roost so long he finally ran away."

We didn't want an argument to ensue, so Rose said, "I agree that Cholerics can be so overbearing that people will want to escape. I admit I've fallen into that weakness myself. But running away is not the answer. Maybe someone in your life or your workplace is stuck in a henpecked position and is about to bolt. The Choleric will simply let the person go and then lament, 'Well, she never did measure up in the first place. Good-bye and good riddance!' Then the Choleric will dive even deeper into their work."

"Phlegmatics, don't you dare rebel or run; put aside your fears and hurt feelings and work it out," I chimed in. "Talk about it. Find a solution; you're a natural mediator. And Cholerics? Stop talking, start listening, and allow the Phlegmatic to have some dignity. You both have weaknesses. Why not start working in your strengths?"

"We may never know their whole story, but it appears that perhaps Jon and Kate were both afraid—for different reasons—to do the hard work of putting their marriage first," Rose said. "Who of us has never been in that same position? Whether you're the company owner or the back room worker, the corporate manager or the team member, or a husband and wife team in a home-based business, success will come only when you're willing to respect and get along with others. And it doesn't really matter who 'rules the roost' in your company—neither of you should be *chicken* about doing a little relationship work!"

How to Work with a Choleric: Quick Tips

Do you see yourself or someone you know in the characteristics of a Choleric? If you're the opposite, Phlegmatic, don't go out and buy your bulletproof vest and body armor yet! The following is a quick-reference list with helpful tips for getting along with and supporting a Choleric leader, employee, client, or co-worker. And if you're a Choleric who runs the show in your home business or workplace, we hope you can use this list to stay working in your strengths instead of your weaknesses. If you do, everyone will be happy to do what you say—and do it your way!

"Next week we'll be learning more about the Melancholies," I concluded. "Do pay attention to the Melancholies you meet and we'll give you time to share your observations next time."

What Did We Learn This Time?

This time we have a helpful reference chart to help you with Cholerics!

How to Help Cholerics at Work
"They're bossier than the boss and think we're all idiots!"

Basic desire	Learn to:
Being in charge	Appreciate the need for decisiveness and leadership in their area of work
Emotional needs	
Loyalty	Don't try to buck them; they will fight for you if you stand by them
Sense of control	Resist the urge to rebel when you feel controlled; they might be right in trying to control you
Appreciation	Don't withhold appreciation; frequently express appropriate thanks
Credit for work	Praise their hard efforts to everyone in the group
Get depressed when	
Some part of their life is out of control	Ask what part of their life is out of control and just listen

Control by	
Threats, intimidation, and a loud voice	Show them other ways of getting people to respond

Best at	
Taking charge easily	Even if they are not the boss, give them some type of authority
Being dynamic and active	Keep them busy but don't let them take over completely
Having a compulsive need for change	Appreciate their desire to keep improving things but tell them not to change things without getting permission
Needing to correct wrongs	Send them in to do battle for the group; they won't let you down
Being strong-willed and decisive	Allow them to call the shots when everyone else is stalled
Being unemotional	Depend on them to do the difficult; they won't overreact
Not being easily discouraged	Appreciate that they don't take problems personally; they like the challenge
Being independent and self-sufficient	Don't micromanage them; allow them reasonable freedom
Exuding confidence	Watch for bravado; ask them to encourage, train, and guide others
Running anything	Don't be afraid to ask them to do new things
Being goal-oriented	Push them to higher production and they will excel
Seeing the whole picture	Lean on them to get the big picture and to chart the best course
Organizing well	Let them plan the program and assign details/duties to others
Seeking practical solutions	Depend on their keen sense of reality to temper pie-in-the-sky dreams
Moving quickly to action	Help others in the workplace appreciate their fast thinking and implementation
Delegating work	Trust their ability to assign duties to others
Insisting on production	Praise them for keeping things moving and accomplishing so much
Making the goal	Make sure you have a realistic reward system in place to keep them going

Stimulating activity	Give them the freedom/authority to motivate others
Thriving on opposition	Tell them they can't do it and watch them go
Having little need for friends	You can leave them alone and know they won't be chatting or visiting
Usually being right	Help them listen and be sensitive to others' suggestions but trust their insight
Excelling in emergencies	Don't try to hold them back; they will "save" the situation; ask how you can help

Presentation style

Authoritative	Don't try to change their style
Convincing	Help them avoid too much aggression

Problems

Too bossy	Remind them of the limits of their assignments and authority
Impatient	Ask them to wait for others, but back them up in the need for deadlines
Quick-tempered	They see no reason everyone should not move and obey; help them understand the different personalities
Can't relax	Don't try to make them slow down, but do invite them to join you in some quiet time
Too impetuous	Don't be afraid to remind them kindly of the last time they acted too quickly, without thinking; they'll get it
Enjoy arguments	They can't resist an invitation to "win"; explain that unnecessary conflict shuts others—and their productivity—down
Come on too strong	Help them match others with tone of voice and pace to create the optimum environment
Inflexible	Ask them to consider yielding on the less-important issues and back them up on the big ones
See tears and emotions as weakness	Remind them that not everyone can be Choleric and help them see others' strengths
Unsympathetic	Since they tend to focus primarily on the task, help them also see the people involved
Don't analyze the details	Keep them working in the big areas and encourage them to get a Melancholy helper

Work may become their god	Watch for too many hours and impending burnout; send them home if necessary
Bored by trivia	When talking to them, quickly get to the point
Tend to use people	Help them see that people are more important than production
Make decisions for others	Have an office seminar about setting and enforcing healthy boundaries
Can't apologize or mouth the words "I'm sorry"	Remind them that they are usually right about the work but sometimes wrong when relating to people
Can do everything better than others	Praise them, but then confront them kindly but firmly, pointing out the valuable contributions of others
Demand loyalty in the ranks	Help them understand loyalty needs to be earned first, and show them how
Know everything	Agree they are smart but inject some humor: challenge them with something they can't possibly know
Intrude on others' space	Teach them to be careful about touching others and to respect physical boundaries
Too independent	Keep them working at least part-time with teams when they are not the leader
Not complimentary	Have them make lists of what others have done that is right and encourage them to *at least* say thanks

With praise, Cholerics will work forever. They think days off are a waste of time.

8

Perfect Personality

Melancholy

From the beginning of our class, Dr. Hastings had been the doubter. He'd come to our "Personality Plus at Work" class only because his mentor, Dr. Hemingway, had insisted he attend and—to use his term—try to "loosen up" a bit. Our doctor had indeed loosened up and had grown to consider us as the family he didn't have. He had become the one who always had a thoughtful question for us.

On what we had proclaimed as our "Melancholy Day," it was no surprise to see him arrive early. As he approached, Florence and I (Rose) noticed how he appeared more relaxed and not so pinched tight. He even looked more handsome. What was different? His eyes. I'd never noticed they were so blue. A moment later, I realized why—he wasn't wearing his glasses.

"No glasses today, Doctor?" Florence asked.

"No, I had Lasik done this week. And I can see. What a difference." He even seemed to stand taller. "You've got me thinking about myself. Not just my personality, but even how I look. I never wear anything that calls undue attention to myself, even though I do like color. I guess my mother was right when she said, 'You are just no fun.'"

"Did she say that when you were a child?" I asked.

"Yes. I was always serious. I preferred to read rather than watch *Captain Kangaroo*. She said that I was not like a real child."

"Well, now you've learned you were born with your personality and you're a brilliant Melancholy."

"I was always smarter than the other kids, but I wasn't popular. No one thought I was fun."

"But I can tell you are going to be fun from here on," I said, with an encouraging smile.

By now the other students had arrived, and we were ready to begin.

"We are dedicating our Melancholy lessons to Carmen and our personal physician," I told everyone and turned back to the doctor. "May we call you Charles?"

He nodded. "Not Chuck, though."

The group settled down, and we went to work.

"One of the observations we've made about Melancholy children is that because they tend to be a little more serious about things, they sometimes mature more quickly than others," Florence began. "Let's all take the word *maturity*: we all grow older, but we don't all grow up."

Maturity in the dictionary is defined as "full growth and development," but we like to define it with a simple outline:

- Accept myself, who I am—my inborn personality.
- Accept responsibility for my own growth.
- Accept blame for my mistakes and stop putting the blame on others.

"Melancholies can be effective leaders in the workplaces, but they are often second-in-command, making sure the ship doesn't run

118

aground," Florence continued. "Everyone knows that the second-in-command is often the one who does all the work, keeps the ship afloat, and receives little of the credit. If you're the second-in-command, you can resent that reality or you can celebrate it."

Melancholy Characteristics

Judy Warren—one of our Personality Trainers—sent us a note about Melancholies and their contributions to the workplace. She wrote:

1. *Melancholies care.* They care deeply and do nothing superficial or trivial. Like stealth spies, they often anticipate hidden problems no one else sees and will be ready for the worst. As the Sanguine sees the best with no facts, the Melancholy focuses on black clouds heavy with facts. They often warn others about the impending gloom and are frequently correct. Often they make great personal sacrifices for the company. And if they are not also Choleric, they have no need to take center stage or steal the spotlight from the "leading man."

> *Melancholies care deeply and do nothing superficial or trivial.*

2. *Maturity matters.* Maturity is the ability to step outside yourself and see and work for the greater common good. The more self-focused people are, the more they will function in their weaknesses. Sure signs of immaturity in Melancholies are *overreaction* to criticism and refusal to take the blame.

Depending on the Second-in-Command

"Immature Melancholies tend to be too worried, too pessimistic, too defensive, and extremely judgmental of others," I said. "They might not openly criticize, as a more extroverted personality would,

119

but they will keep a record of your imperfections. On the other hand, when they get beyond themselves, see your point, and open up to you, they will be loyal to the death. If you've been blessed with the gift of being a Melancholy, the rest of us want to thank you for the times you've been our greatest second-in-command. We all need you!"

Immature Melancholies tend to be too worried, too pessimistic, too defensive, and extremely judgmental of others.

Other personalities who are working out of their weaknesses will have reactions to difficult situations that are as problematic as those of the Melancholies.

Sanguines who are immature will automatically blame someone else for what has happened. They get upset when they don't get their own way and someone stops all the fun. But they will soon forget and hold no grudges because they can't remember who said what. They quickly move back to self-focus and happiness.

Cholerics are critical, too, but they usually bark about it, try to fix it, make the offenders look stupid, and then move on. They don't hold on to a record of wrongs—there's too much more in life to do than remember all that! But don't think you can try that trick again.

Phlegmatics really don't care that much about what went wrong; they are confident that others will take care of it. If not, a mature Phlegmatic will rise to the occasion just long enough to solve the problem as effectively and quickly as possible. Then he will go back to a comfortable routine and apparent indifference.

They Don't Need to Know

"Rose, why don't you share what Nancy emailed us last week," Florence suggested. I nodded and read to the class:

I travel and speak as part of my work with the Amarillo Women's Network. AWN is a premier source of information, resources, contacts, and opportunities to assist businesswomen. Their website reads, "Networking is not a new idea. Networking is as simple as telling one another about employment and business opportunities. . . ." So don't you think it would be natural that I would be required to make as many contacts with as many people as possible? It comes naturally to me because I'm Sanguine. But not everyone thinks that way. Unhappy introverts—like Melancholies—usually like to be left alone and can't even imagine someone going out to intrude like that on others. I've had many Melancholy people tell me, "Oh, Nancy, not everyone needs to know."

Thanks to the personalities, I know that Melancholies and Phlegmatics normally prefer to work behind the scenes, but they need to understand and appreciate the gifts of us extroverts (Cholerics and Sanguines). The naysayers may bother me a bit, but I don't let them stop me. I've shared my business opportunities in elevators, stores, and even at a large wedding reception in Hawaii!

No Surprises, Please

If you are thinking about throwing a surprise party for someone at work, you might want to think again. Not everyone appreciates surprises.

While we were writing this book, Florence reminded me how oblivious Sanguines can be to the fact that most Melancholies hate surprises. Florence's daughter Marita once threw a big surprise party for her Melancholy husband, Chuck. After Marita had planned the gala event and filled the home with family and friends, Chuck walked in, looked around at all the happy people yelling "Surprise!" went upstairs to his room, and shut the door. He stayed there for an hour and then made a quiet reentry into the group. By then even the Sanguines had caught on to his mood and the party took a quiet turn, ending up more like a funeral than a celebration.

121

I told Florence I could top that "surprise" story. Years ago I dated Melancholy-Phlegmatic Bill, whose birthday was approaching. I'd asked if he wanted a party. "No!" he insisted, but he chuckled after he said it, and I took that as an indirect yes. I wasn't really listening. I was already making the guest list in my head, had the cake picked out, and was deciding what color and theme I would choose for the decorations.

The night of his big surprise birthday party, we went to the restaurant and walked into the back room that I'd decorated so colorfully in a Mexican fiesta theme that afternoon. All his friends shouted, "Surprise!" He seemed stunned but happy to see everyone, and I was pretty proud of myself. I sat down with the guests and started chatting and didn't even notice he'd taken a seat at the far opposite end of the long table. He stayed at that one spot all night, while I walked around to each guest and thanked them for coming. At the end of the evening, after everyone else had left, Bill and I packed his presents into his car, and then I assumed I would follow him home to spend some time winding down after the night's events. I knew he would praise me for a very special evening.

But that's not what happened. Instead, he got in his car and quickly drove away without saying a word: no thanks, no smile, and no joy.

My Sanguine side was immediately crushed, and I started to run after him in my high heels, calling his name. But my Choleric kicked in and I thought, *No* way *is he going to run out on me after all I did for him*! I drove like a maniac to his house. When I got there, I could see him through the window, already in his living room.

He saw me as I walked up to the door, and his big dog, Annie, knew I was there. She was up on her hind legs, nose pressed against the glass, wagging her tail. She loved me. But when I got to the door, I heard Bill on the other side turn the lock with a loud *click*.

I grabbed the knob and turned it frantically, again calling his name. Then I went to the window and looked at him with a silent and pathetic plea. He came to the window and, now only a foot away on the other side of the glass and still looking me straight in the face, closed the curtains and shut me out.

The show was over. I had enough dignity left to get in my car and drive home, sobbing all the way. As a typical introvert, he suffered in silence through the party, all the while planning his exit. He'd put in his time and that was enough. Since I'd failed to listen to him, I didn't deserve anymore, and he let me know it.

It didn't matter how much fun he'd had that night or what other qualities he may have genuinely appreciated about me, he was *not* going to thank me. His Melancholy side was going to punish me for not listening to him in the first place, and his Phlegmatic side avoided conflict by finding a way to make me disappear.

"I know there is no excuse for how he treated me that night, but I also learned that I had a significant part in it by pushing my plans for a party and going against his wishes," I concluded. "I've since learned to listen better and to honor the requests for time, space, and privacy of the introverted temperaments. And of course, I will never plan anything unexpected for a Melancholy again. Ever."

"Boy, that must have been humiliating," said Fran.

"It was, Fran, but I went shopping afterward—a little retail therapy—and felt much better."

Fran and the others laughed.

Meticulous Care

Then Florence told about her Melancholy son-in-law, Chuck, who'd worked as a photographer for the San Diego Police Department. There he learned all the tricks that burglars use to break into houses. He was already security conscious, but his time observing creative crime opened his eyes and mind to the new possibilities. To protect his garage full of his treasures, he devised some protective measures. He bought a transmitter with a remote control from Radio Shack, drilled a hole in the cement floor of the garage, and chained a huge bolt to the bottom of the door. When he backs out, he presses button number 1, which closes the door, then button number 2, which makes the bolt plunge into the hole.

"Now, if you and I got this far in our plans for protection, we'd think we were brilliant, but what we don't know is that full-time burglars have remotes in their vans and they drive up and down our streets pressing their buttons," Florence explained. "Sooner or later a garage door that happens to have that code will pop open. Unless some neighborhood sleuth is looking out the window, the burglars will have all the televisions in the van in minutes, press the button to close the door, and be on their way. When the owners get home, they will suspect nothing until they sit down to watch television."

Because of this, Chuck added a third button that turns off the electricity in the garage, foiling the crooks. When Chuck comes home at night, he presses his buttons. First, he turns on the electricity, then raises the bolt, and then opens the door—happy to know that his twelve motorcycles are still safe.

Later, Chuck and Marita bought a large home in a small town. The living room is two and a half stories high with a bedroom jutting out over it like an oversized balcony. In one corner of this spacious living room, Marita has created her office. There is a wrought-iron antique gate that blocks off the two desks and cabinets where she works. Piles of papers, open books, and overflowing wastebaskets are partially hidden in this corner.

Chuck has protected the house—which is out in the woods on a ten-acre lot—by connecting a system to the local police. Also he has a camera that is activated when the alarm is triggered.

We all make fun of Chuck's hypervigilance, but one day he was vindicated. When he and Marita were out, robbers kicked in the front door, set off the alarm, and were filmed racing through the room in search of treasures. When the police came to confer with Chuck, one officer spotted Marita's corner, went over to inspect the damage, and called out excitedly, "I've found what they did. They totally ransacked this part of the house!"

Chuck looked over and calmly answered, "No, that's the way it looks all the time. My wife likes to work in confusion."

Reluctance to Praise

One of the biggest yet most unaddressed problems is the Melancholy's reluctance to praise or thank others when the job isn't yet perfect or finished. Years ago—before we understood and taught the personalities—Florence asked her husband, Fred, why he couldn't compliment her on what she was doing. He answered her, "Because it's not done right yet!" Sanguines need praise to keep them going or they won't continue. If you're a Melancholy who works with a Sanguine, assume you are praising the portion of the work that is finished and hope for more progress in the future.

Remember, Melancholies, we all applaud your high standards, we thank you for saving our necks at crucial times, and we hope someday to get a little closer to perfection.

How to Work with a Melancholy: Quick Tips

Did you recognize the marks of a perfect Melancholy in the above stories? If so, what will you do if you realize you work with a Melancholy? If you're the opposite, Sanguine, don't burst into tears yet! The following is a quick-reference list with helpful tips for getting along with and supporting a Melancholy customer, client, co-worker, employee, or boss. And if you're the Melancholy person in charge of shaping up those imperfect people in your workplace, please use this list to stay focused on your strengths and not your weaknesses. If you do, your office will run perfectly, like a well-oiled machine, and everyone will be grateful.

What Did We Learn This Time?

This time we have a helpful reference chart to help you with Melancholies!

How to Help Melancholies at Work
"They're such busybodies, criticizing everything!"

Basic desire	Learn to:
Perfection	Appreciate their need for high standards and the pursuit of excellence
Emotional needs	
Sensitivity	Be aware of easily hurt feelings; don't joke around; they need understanding
Support	They will sacrifice for you or the company; let them know you support them
Space	Be flexible in giving them time and space to complete the job; they want to do it right
Silence	Work to create a quiet space for them; move the Sanguines if you have to
Get depressed when	
No one understands them	Ask them to explain; then really listen and ask questions
Control by	
Threats of moods	Don't buy into the drama or depression; ask instead how to solve the problem
Best at	
Being deep and thoughtful	Assign them to the "think tank" and the new ideas department
Analyzing carefully	Rely on their natural ability to see potential problems; have them test ideas or plans
Being serious and purposeful	Don't try to lighten them up; appreciate their depth; don't laugh at them
Being prone to genius	Understand and allow for their depth to go to the limit, benefiting everyone
Being talented and creative	Expect and appreciate that they will think outside the box
Being artistic or musical	Put them where they can use their vision for story, color, design, sound, music, art

Being philosophical	Rely on their talents to harmonize the inter-personal into the production
Appreciating beauty	Allow them to bring appropriate but unusual or unique touches into the workplace
Being sensitive to others	Make sure they don't get too enmeshed in the problems of their co-workers
Being self-sacrificing	Don't gush but give sincere praise for their extra efforts
Being conscientious	Put them in charge of the things that must be done perfectly and on time
Being idealistic	Don't put them down for having goals, ideas, or impossible dreams
Being schedule-oriented	Let them work from charts, graphs, and schedules and have them help the Phlegmatics and Sanguines with scheduling
Being a perfectionist	Understand that their perfectionism may be exactly what you need
Having high ideals	Watch for arrogance but thank them for their brilliance and inspiration
Being deeply creative	Some Melancholies are so focused on their creativity, they don't notice the clutter around them—allow them a *little* mess
Being organized, neat, and tidy	Some Melancholies are so organized, you should put them in charge of keeping things going perfectly
Economical	They may tend to be tightwads, but do put them in charge of the money
Seeing the problems	Don't consider them naysayers and listen to their well-thought-out warnings
Finding creative solutions	If you ask them to come up with a better solution, they usually will
Needing to finish the job	Expect some distress when they can't spend enough time getting a perfect result; help them let go when necessary
Having deep compassion for others	Rely on their genuine caring to help solve the office personality problems
Being loyal "to the death"	Earn their trust and respect first and you'll have their loyalty for life

127

Presentation style	
Accurate with facts	Help them avoid getting lost in the details
Sincere at heart	Don't try to change their style

Problems	
Remembering the negatives	Have an office seminar on the problem with grudges and the power of forgiveness
Being moody and depressed	Affirm their mood; don't try to change it but do ask them to limit their acting out in the workplace
Enjoying being the victim	Don't let them blame others; call them to the higher standard they already know
False humility and self-deprecation	Affirming them in a quiet, understanding way often stops some of the emotional drama
Tending to hypochondria and knowing the latest disease	Expect that their fears will show up in frequent illnesses; go to them if you feel sick— they'll know what's wrong.
Being too introspective	Praise their depth but ask them to help you see and work with the big picture in view
Talking about all the details and tragedies	In the same way you limit the Sanguine storyteller, try to limit the Melancholy's discussion of unnecessary drama
Aiming too high	Help them avoid depression by being realistic about their goals
Hesitant to start projects	They worry from the beginning about reaching perfection; give them a plan
Tending to be withdrawn and remote	They need time to nurse wounds, but don't let them overindulge in self-pity
Critical of others	Affirm their keen eye but ask them to give workable solutions instead of criticism
Holding back affection	Try to touch their deep feelings and explain that praise and warmth are necessary for the good of others
Suspicious of others	Thank them for looking out for problems; help them see others' good intentions
Seeking vengeance	Reassure them that you will make every effort to fight for justice in the workplace so they don't have to
Skeptical of praise	Make sure your compliments are genuine and given sincerely, preferably in private

Deep need for approval	Don't let their vanity or pride keep you from giving them authentic praise
Hard to please	Assure them you value their high standards and ask that they loosen them a bit for others
Preferring analysis to work	They can tend to stay cerebral; gently call them back to earth
Spending too much time planning	Understand they get their greatest pleasure in the planning; give them a deadline
Depressed over imperfections	Reassure them you do not expect them to be perfect all the time; expect that they may impose this on themselves
Can be vain	Praise their accomplishments and then ask them to work on helping others
Socially insecure	Understand that their vanity may be a façade and they need genuine understanding

Recognize that a Melancholy's ability to spot problems may be an asset for you, but don't let him or her get carried away with the tragedies.

9

Peaceful Personality

Phlegmatic

"Rose, may I speak with you privately for a minute?"

I (Rose) stepped outside the classroom with Darlene Guttenberg, and she got *right to the point*. (My father would have liked her.)

"You know I'm Choleric and my husband, Hans, is Phlegmatic. It doesn't take a rocket scientist to tell that. But he's just been going along with you all in the group, and I think he secretly believes he's Choleric, no matter what I say. How can I change that?"

"Darlene, I understand. There are many Phlegmatic men—by no means lazy slouches or unsuccessful in their work—who stubbornly refuse to admit they are Phlegmatic. Frequently after I give a personality presentation, a Phlegmatic man will amble up cautiously to where I am speaking with others, hold back patiently until everyone else is finished talking, and then—staying a few feet away from me—whisper meekly, 'Hi, I'm a powerful Choleric, just like you.'"

Darlene laughed. "What do you do when that happens?"

"Well, in the past I've tended to be a little arrogant. *Really*! I'd think, as I give him the once-over and see classic Phlegmatic casual clothes; a stolid, droopy expression on his face; and his lean toward me. He continues to stare at me, *waiting* for me to take over. With my arms folded across my chest, my high heels firmly planted in the carpet, and my lips pursed, I'd think, *Yeah, right, Mister, and the moon is made of green cheese!*"

Darlene nodded as if to admit she shared that same tendency to Choleric arrogance.

"But then I remember that he's been shaped by the culture—or his henpecking wife—never to admit a soft side. Probably he needs to believe that he is an 'alpha dog' and that others will see him as a man's man. When a Phlegmatic man feels inadequate—for whatever reason—he needs the Choleric mask. When he's confident and assured, he can throw it away. This man needs my respect, and in my Choleric arrogance I am refusing to give it to him. So I've learned to take a slow, deep breath and get in touch with a more mature version of myself, one who can reach down inside, grab some genuine compassion, and practice what she preaches. That's when I can flash a sweet smile, touch his hand gently, and say, 'Hi, I'm so glad you enjoyed the talk. Is this your wife?' and I change the subject."

Darlene looked at me. "You said *henpecking wife*."

"Yes, henpecking wife. Darlene, all Phlegmatics need respect, especially from their spouses. We must stop caricaturing them as couch potatoes. Our culture—especially in the workplace—promotes macho men and makes sensitive men look like sissies. We have to counter that. Phlegmatics are powerful in their own way, and many are hardworking leaders in the community, wealthy entrepreneurs, tireless saints working for the poor, and heads of nations. We're going to spend our day going over the strengths of the Phlegmatic today, so pay close attention." I smiled and reached out, took her arm, and led her back into the room.

"Take it from me—one Choleric to another. The world could not survive without the strengths of the Phlegmatic."

Phlegmatic Characteristics

Choleric traits are clearly what our culture has defined as "masculine." Phlegmatic strengths seem decidedly "feminine" by cultural standards, and so it's common for Phlegmatic men to stubbornly insist they are *not* Phlegmatic. No man or his wife really wants him to be weak, wimpy Mr. Nice Guy.

Choleric Strengths	Phlegmatic Strengths
Bold	Gentle
Adventurous	Adaptable
Self-reliant	Submissive
Outspoken	Obliging
Forceful	Diplomatic
Animated	Reserved
Decisive	Friendly
Mover	Patient
Leader	Supportive
Chief	Contented
Productive	Consistent
Promoter	Pleasant

Often "real men" are conditioned to be brute sports enthusiasts or insensitive louts with beefy biceps and bulging wallets. As a result, the sensitive, creative, or genius Melancholy-Phlegmatic men may find themselves trying to walk with a strut, talking louder than they have to, or getting angry to assert themselves.

But all of us know a husband, brother, son, father, or friend who is Phlegmatic or Melancholy and is still very masculine. There is nothing wrong with him, and he is exactly the way God made him. And when a Phlegmatic man is gentle, for example, it is a

132

much different gentleness than feminine softness. In other words, men are still men and women are still women, but they *can* share temperaments, just as the sexes can have the same blood type or hair color.

We've already talked about the problem of cherry-picking personality traits, wanting certain ones to be ours. I know a Phlegmatic-Melancholy man who swears he is Choleric because he checked "strong-willed" on the personality profile (included in the back of this book) when in reality he is a stubborn Phlegmatic. For some emotional reason—probably a Choleric wife!—he does *not* want to be a Phlegmatic. He also thinks he is Choleric because he checked "outspoken." But when a Phlegmatic has waited long enough to feel comfortable in his surroundings and the people he's with, he will have no trouble speaking his mind.

Phlegmatics can provide strong, steady leadership that might even surpass that of the Cholerics.

He also checked "adventurous" on the profile because he was the first of his friends to bungee jump at the state fair—but he's afraid to make a lucrative career move his wife has nagged him about for the last five years. Everyone has moments of being adventurous, but some have to think about it first, and some have to plan it out for months.

If you are the breadwinner for your family or a manager at work, does that automatically make you Choleric? Not really. Many of the world's leaders—including American presidents Gerald R. Ford and George Bush Sr.—have been brilliant, balanced Phlegmatic men. When Phlegmatics have had time to check things out and feel safe in a situation, they often assume leadership. But the *real* Choleric has already swept the room, decided the challenge is too small—or the people are idiots—and has left for something he thinks is bigger and better.

Phlegmatics can provide strong, steady leadership that might even surpass that of the Cholerics. When the Choleric sees that most of the work has been done satisfactorily, and she can leave someone reasonably intelligent to wrap things up, she will probably leave early and go to the next big project. But the faithful Phlegmatic will stay until the job is completely finished and the janitor has gone home. Remember that the real Choleric can be abrupt and hurtful, while the natural Phlegmatic is inoffensive and kind.

Looking for the Easier Way

Tammy Bennett is our dear friend and co-instructor when we give the "Upper Class" seminars. The three of us—Florence, Rose, and Tammy—are quite a Choleric trio. Tammy's husband, Ed, is a Phlegmatic who has risen to the top in his profession because of his engineering expertise and easy-to-get-along-with disposition.

Tammy says, "He gives his all at work and collapses when he gets home. I have to give him projects or he would just take naps."

Recently when they were moving from one city to another, Ed came home to help Tammy pack. She asked him to empty the gas out of the power mower and other garden equipment so they could be shipped.

He agreed, "No problem." It was the season for college basketball finals, and when Tammy thought he was out in the garage, she discovered him in his easy chair watching the games on television.

"When are you going to empty the gas?" she asked.

"It's underway. Don't worry."

Tammy went back to her packing but kept checking to see when he was going to drain out the gas. All he did was go to the front door, open it, stick his head out, and sit back down. She could tell he hadn't done a thing. She knew what a job it was to drain those machines, as she'd done it herself last time they had moved, when he was too busy at work to come home and help her. When she came to get Ed back on task, he was smiling, relaxed, and enjoying the game.

"When are you going to do the gas job?" Tammy asked again. "It's getting dark out!"

Ed motioned her away with a wave of his hand and went back to the game. Tammy was not happy, and she did what she'd been doing throughout their marriage for thirty years. "Then I'll just do it myself!" she said. She opened the front door—and there in the driveway were the power lawn mower, the blower, and the edger. Their motors were all running, and one was sputtering off. "What is this?" she yelled over the sound of the game.

Ed looked up and said, "It's an easy job. All you do is turn the motors on and let them sit there until they use up the gas. One's about done." He was pleased with himself and couldn't understand how she could possibly be upset with his clever Phlegmatic solution.

As Tammy told me this story she added, "But the worst part was, when our son called, Ed told him he was exhausted from the whole day of hard work in the garage, draining out the gas from the equipment. He told his son, 'I was just trying to keep your mother happy, but she got mad at me anyway.'" Their son felt sorry for his father, and Ed went back to the game.

If you're a high-powered Choleric who is ready to blow off steam, consider that the low-key Phlegmatic might be able to show you *an easier way to work*!

Finding a Better Way

Tammy shared another story about how Ed wanted to have a garden at their new home, so Tammy planted a few flowers in the backyard.

One Saturday, when Ed was home from work, she asked him if he'd go out and weed the little patch. He agreed cheerfully and headed outside. Later Tammy looked out to see how her husband was doing and saw him lying on a chaise lounge cushion that he'd taken off the chair and put on the ground between the rows in the garden. He was lying down on his side, propped up on one elbow, his lemonade nearby, and he was slowly and carefully pulling out the crabgrass in front of him.

"Are you taking a nap?" she yelled.

"No, I've invented a new way to weed. You lie down and pull up all the weeds you can reach. Then you move the pillow and start again."

Tammy and I both marveled at how Ed could combine weeding and resting—and think he'd been working.

Though the stories about Ed seem comical, they actually reveal Phlegmatic strengths: the ability to find a quicker, easier way to do things and a cooperative spirit. Here are some of the reasons we need to appreciate Phlegmatics, especially if they are the men in our workplace:

Phlegmatic men need to know that others appreciate the gift of their temperament. Others in their lives (mothers, sweethearts, wives, employers) need to stop trying to make them over into the type of man *they* want.

Phlegmatic men can make excellent leaders in the home, community, and workplace when they have overcome emotional fears and drawn on their solid strengths of patience, determination, perseverance, and their ability to listen to others before making big decisions.

Phlegmatic leaders may not move as quickly as real Cholerics, but they can be just as—or even more—effective. They may not work harder, but they just may work *smarter*!

No More Major Meltdowns

We told the class some more stories from people who had written to us. Sandy, a sweet Sanguine-Phlegmatic, has been a conference director for twenty years. At first, she loved the idea because of the people she'd be helping, but soon she found herself overwhelmed, overworked, and definitely having no fun. "My initial role was to plan the conferences, inventory the books, tape the lectures, duplicate the tapes, oversee the room assignments, and keep everyone happy all day long."

Sandy has the Phlegmatic strength of a kind, caring spirit for people and a winning way with her Sanguine smile. "But I'm not wired for details," Sandy shared. "Often at the product tables, it would all cave in on me at once, and I'd have a major meltdown. I was completely overwhelmed!"

So she decided to hire an assistant to help her with the organization. Not knowing the personalities, Sandy hired a Sanguine who "was fun to be with but really no help at all. She just wanted to take the microphone out of my hand all the time!"

When Sandy discovered the personality principles in *Personality Plus*, she had the solution. "I hired a mother-daughter team; one is a peaceful Phlegmatic who can weather the crises that come up and can calm down difficult people. The other is a perfect Melancholy who doesn't need to be up front and enjoys keeping everything perfectly organized. They are both the behind-the-scenes support I needed!

"When I arrive at a conference now," shares Sandy, "they hand me a notebook that has the schedule, room assignments, room names, and all the details—even the names of the bus drivers. That frees me up to be with the people. I now have the time to establish relationships with them, from calling before the conference to encourage them, to loving on them when they arrive. Now I get to work in my strengths—no more major meltdowns!"

Let the Structure Speak

Fran asked, "Florence, how do you deal with the Phlegmatic who is given lots of time and space and still doesn't perform? We have someone like that in our corporate office."

Florence told her about our friend Carol, a Choleric who had successfully dealt with the same problem. "Carol used to nag and threaten but she stopped. It was only driving her crazy and driving others away. She found a better way by setting clear boundaries—and consequences—ahead of time. Her motto is 'Let the structure speak.'"

"What do you mean?" asked Fran.

"Most Phlegmatics are faithful at following clear instructions and doing something exactly the way it needs to be done. A mature Phlegmatic doesn't resent orders and directions but rather appreciates them," Florence explained. "They need someone to lead them and something to follow, but that 'thing' doesn't have to be a person who constantly reminds (nags), checks up on her, yells, screams, or threatens. When a Phlegmatic is criticized, they will clam up and tune out. It's over!"

A mature Phlegmatic doesn't resent orders and directions but appreciates them.

"Boy, you can say that again!" said Darlene. Hans just stared ahead.

I added, "This approach works. Here's a perfect example: when you tell your Phlegmatic employee they need to finish a task, also give them helpful instructions—where to get assistance and, more importantly, a deadline. But deadlines alone aren't enough. People need to know the consequence if that deadline is not met, like having to stay late until it's done, giving up a Saturday, or losing out on the bonus. Now the structure is in place—task, specific instructions, help, Monday morning deadline, consequence—and it 'speaks' for itself."

"What if they wait until the very last minute to do the work?"

"You have to pick your battles. Don't get upset if the job was not tackled until Sunday night, as long as it's on your desk Monday morning!"

How to Work with a Phlegmatic: Quick Tips

Even though you've read a few examples of how easy life can be when you understand the practices of a peaceful Phlegmatic, you may still need some tips on how to work with a Phlegmatic. If you're the opposite, Choleric, don't worry: just slow down, take a deep breath, and count to ten . . . or one hundred. Not only can we help you respect the Phlegmatic, but with the quick-reference list and helpful tips below, you'll be able to get along with and support your Phlegmatic leader, client, employee, or co-worker. And if you're a Phlegmatic who's in an overwhelming workplace, we hope you can use this list to stay working in your strengths instead of your weaknesses. If you do, all your career problems will be small ones!

What Did We Learn This Time?

This time we have a helpful reference chart to help you with Phlegmatics!

How to Help Phlegmatics at Work
"They're so nice but they never finish anything!"

Basic desire	Learn to:
Peace	Appreciate the stability and calm (no high drama) they bring to the workplace
Emotional needs	
Peace and quiet	Understand they will work harder and smarter in a clean, quiet space
Feeling of worth	Look past their slower pace and let them know what you appreciate about them
Lack of stress	Uphold clear deadlines but don't nag or threaten
Respect from co-workers	Let them know they are necessary to the team even if they produce the least
Get depressed when	
No one values them or they get overwhelmed	Appreciate the intangibles they bring to the workplace, not just what they produce
Control by	
Procrastination	Don't let them push the work onto others by their hesitation

Best at	
Making sure the group is comfortable	Put them on the hospitality committee
Always finding a middle ground	Ask what they think and then thank them
Staying calm when there is a crisis	Ask them to help console or calm others; thank them for their stability
Don't overreact to a negative situation	Invite their ideas for bringing some balance to the problem
Having a low-key personality	Appreciate their inoffensiveness
Seeing with a balanced view	Appreciate their lack of extreme or unrealistic responses
Patience	Put them in a support position to help those who tend to overreact
Having a consistent life	Appreciate that you always know what to expect from them
Being quiet but witty	Let them know you appreciate their humor
Being sympathetic and kind	Ask them to keep an eye on others who need their nurturing or support
Being happily reconciled to life	Thank them for their realistic expectations at work
Being adaptable	Appreciate their flexibility but don't keep them in an area that's not their strength
Being competent	Appreciate their intelligence and skills, even when they may not seem obvious
Being peaceful and agreeable	Put them in a strong support position where they can follow a strong leader
Mediating problems	Confer authority on them as mediators and let them rest afterward
Standing up under pressure	Let them have time and space to reenergize afterward and thank them publicly
Finding the easy way	Stay open to the possibility that their easy way is the best way for all
Being a capable administrator	Put them in charge of others who will do the actual work; they'll help keep the peace
Being an accurate observer	Invite them to share their observations for improving the workplace
Listening well	Place them in areas where they can discern best how to serve others' needs

140

Avoiding conflicts	Rely on them to avoid or not fuel high-drama situations
Having many friends	Appoint them as liaison or company representative
Having compassion and concern	Make sure they're working in an area where they can consistently help others

Presentation style

Believable	Appreciate their honesty
Resist hype	Help them add a little color to the talk

Problems

Lack of enthusiasm	Don't expect them to be the major motivator; they're better as support persons
Are fearful and worried	When they get easily overwhelmed, give them clear and simple direction
Indecisive	When they see the whole world of possibilities, help them with limits or deadlines in making decisions
Avoiding responsibility	They fear conflict or pressure; set up a system where these are minimized
Stubbornness	Determine what is making them freeze up and help solve the underlying problem
Selfishness	If they're avoiding conflict or pressure, help them open up to others
May be too shy	Help them identify the fear that is making them withdraw; sometimes it's just a lazy habit
May be too compromising	Compromise is a way to avoid pressure or conflict; help them overcome fear with facts
Can be self-righteous	Help them see that the loud, bossy ones have strengths too
Not goal-oriented	If they get indecisive and overwhelmed, help them set up smaller, manageable goals
Lack of self-motivation	Find out what does motivate them and zero in on that; pair them with motivators
Resent being pushed	Be aware of resentment under the pleasant surface; reaffirm their worth and authority
Can be lazy and careless	Don't allow others to clean up their mess; hold them accountable
Prefer to watch rather than work	Be specific about activities they need to do and have them make a list and check off completed tasks

Making excuses	Use the Oreo approach: *reassure, correct, thank*
Indifference to plans	Ask them to think about and name the benefits of the plans
Keeping emotions bottled up	Make appointments for regular times to draw out their true feelings or needs
Discouraging others	Help them identify the fear that is making them hold others back
Remaining uninvolved	They may not get involved unless you give them specific directions, so do it
Judging others	Bring them back to their ability for balance and help them see the good in others
Can be sarcastic	Understand they're feeling out of control or are holding anger in; have a private talk later
Resisting change	Ask for their input and identify the rewards of change that might genuinely interest them

Phlegmatics might not say much, but they are waiting for you to ask for their valuable input. Do it!

PART 3

THE PERSONALITIES IN SPECIAL WORKING RELATIONSHIPS

10

Personalities in Spousal Partnerships

As we gathered for the start of our third unit on the personalities in specific jobs, Howard came up to Rose and me and said, "I don't see how anyone in any job can really do well without an understanding of the personalities. I'm amazed I got as far as I did, but I can already see what a difference this has started to make in my restaurant. Thank you."

"You're welcome," we both said.

Howard had been the most pompous of anyone in the class at the beginning. He'd been likable, sociable, and successful, but at times there just seemed to be too much of Howard. During our time together he had toned down, seen his weaknesses, and even lost weight. He'd found a soul mate in Carmen, and he was starting a whole new life.

Encouraged by Howard's progress, I (Florence) began our session by explaining how knowledge of the personalities had changed my ability to work with my husband, Fred, and then Rose told my story from her perspective.

"I remember the day when I was sitting with Fred in their kitchen. Florence was on the phone, and Fred got up to do the dishes while he and I talked about married couples working together. I'd observed how Fred and Florence had both learned to focus on each other's strengths, so I said, 'Fred, I think couples today look at each other the wrong way.'"

Fred was always good about dropping whatever he was doing, facing the person who was speaking with him, and giving them his full attention. "Okay, Rose, tell me what you mean," he said.

"Well, for many years now I have been helping with the singles and divorced groups in my church. They all say they want to meet a nice person, but no one ever seems to make a good connection, and the ones who start dating never seem to last. I think people rush into relationships, ignoring the practical issues, and then after the wedding decide to spend the rest of their life running their spouse through the mill."

Fred nodded. He and Florence had spent many years counseling couples who struggled with problems.

"While they are dating they see each other through rose-colored glasses, and then after they marry, they start looking at each other through magnifying glasses," I said.

He chuckled. "You're right, Rose."

"But that's just wrong," I continued. "It should be the other way around. Before marriage, put them under the microscope. Check them out for major weaknesses. But after the wedding, put on those rose-colored glasses and always see their strengths!"

A few members of the class chuckled and nodded. "Fred liked that, too, and told me so," Rose said. "And I miss him. He always listened so attentively and never said, 'Get to the point, Rosie; get to the point.'"

I added, "Rose is right. Fred and I both had each other under the microscope—before we studied personalities. This morning, let's begin by reviewing some of the problems between spouses

146

who work together. Maybe by now some of you can see that it's often the perfectionist, critical Melancholy and the easily wounded, childlike Sanguine who struggle with this the most. They can be more dramatic than the Choleric-Phlegmatic partners."

A Good Team

Why does the Melancholy take pleasure in pointing out mistakes? Sometimes he is resentful of the Sanguine's social appeal—while feeling he is doing all of the work, or at least the only one doing it correctly. I was sitting with such a couple, Pam and Bob, at a convention recently. They are very successful in their business and asked for my evaluation of them. I'd noticed that several times, while she (a Sanguine) had been charming their friends, he (a Melancholy) had corrected her loose facts. I asked him if he noticed what he'd been doing in slipping in his corrections. He hadn't, and then I suggested he was quietly putting her down to get some attention away from her. I explained that Fred and I had been like him and his wife, and I told them our story.

Fred and I sat down one night, at my insistence. I promised to give him an hour to tell me his complaints and then I would have my time. We agreed we'd each share our opinions and that the other would not interrupt. Fred had no trouble pointing out that I talked too much and was too loud. He said that often he felt left out. Sometimes he'd try to tell a funny story but it wouldn't come out the way I had previously told it. His Melancholy nature was hurt.

So I agreed that I would tell only one story, even when two came to my mind. Instead of being the butt of my humor, I'd try to make him the hero of some of my stories. And I'd work on toning down my volume. In turn, he'd never again interrupt or correct me in front of people. He could write my errors down on his ever-present three-by-five cards. Everything I'd said or done wrong should be noted, and each Monday night we'd sit down amiably and review my mistakes.

The first Monday he had quite a list. I paid attention, jotted them down, and sincerely started to work on improving. He hadn't interrupted me all week, so I had no complaints. The next Monday he had only a short list, and by the third week he had no corrections at all.

One of Fred's complaints was that I never knew people's names. I said I had a poor memory. He told me I had an amazing memory. "It's just that you don't ask their names because you don't need to know," he said. "They are just part of your worldwide audience and as long as they pay attention, that's all you need."

I thought this was a harsh analysis, but from then on when I would see Fred coming toward me at a social function, I'd grab my little audience and say, "Your name, honey. Quick! Your name!" He'd come over and ask nicely, "What is your new friend's name?" Sometimes I would have forgotten it that quickly, but I did begin to see that Fred was right. As I became aware of my failures of talking too much and not listening, I pledged to change and I became a better and more respected communicator. Fred agreed never to correct me again in front of anyone, unless what I was saying would start an international conflagration. And finally I learned to listen.

As I told these stories of my own failures to Pam and Bob, they both listened. (I have learned that people get the point better when you are able to make the problem yours and not blame them.) Pam explained that she had been in the business before she married Bob, and she assumed he would be as excited as she was about the constant party atmosphere. But he didn't like social gatherings and preferred to stay home and do the accounting. They had already figured this much out before they heard me speak, but each one was quietly unhappy with the other. Learning about the personalities in a humorous way had opened up a new avenue of communication for them, and they were already dividing up their workload in a positive manner.

But there was still a little bite to their conversation. He was still unhappy with her need for center stage, and she didn't like his quiet sniping. That night he saw for the first time what he had been doing, and she was overjoyed at his desire to limit his complaints. Telling the stories of how Fred and I had to change gave them a picture of themselves. As an intelligent couple, they were able to adapt quickly. He stopped nitpicking and that made her happy.

Sanguine women are very easy to cheer up. Don't correct them. Tell them they are beautiful, be pleasant at parties, and do as much of the real work as possible. They will love you.

A Beautiful Balance

I met a business couple from South Africa, Imraan (the Choleric husband) and Shahana (the Phlegmatic wife), at a recent convention after I spoke. Later they sent me this email:

> It has been an interesting journey for us as a family and as business owners. First of all, our exposure to the personalities has helped tremendously in understanding and accepting each other. As a couple we have learned to focus on each other's strengths in working our business. We share the workload and accept that the "expert" in that field will do the task at hand. However, we don't limit ourselves, either. Over time, we've both benefitted by trying to develop some of the strengths of the other. It creates a beautiful balance.
>
> Before understanding the personalities, we used to think that our differences were reason enough to argue—and used to try desperately to change each other. Once we understood personalities, we could celebrate our differences and not assume that our spouse was deliberately trying to irritate us. We are so grateful for the study of the personalities and how it has opened our eyes and hearts to these valuable insights in human behavior. It continues to benefit us and so many people in South Africa.

That reminded me of the time Fred and I decided to share responsibilities in our speaking business, too. We'd already divided our workload. Fred made all the hotel, airline, restaurant, and transportation plans. He kept charts of our airline miles, travel status, and redemption levels. He made the phone calls to confirm speaking dates, places, and times. He negotiated my fees and kept track of expenses. Fred shipped our books to the event, set up and manned the book table, kept track of sales and inventory, shipped leftover books back home, and counseled men and women in the hallways during the event breaks. At home he continued to take good care of me, cooking gourmet meals and making sure the household ran smoothly. I know it sounds to some of you Melancholies like I didn't do anything, but I wrote the books and did the speaking. That should count for something! Right?

The problem was that during the times I wasn't onstage or writing, I would often check on Fred to make sure he was doing things right. This only irritated Fred, and we would get into arguments. One day, before I was to go up onstage and give a personality presentation, Fred pulled me aside and asked me to look out over the auditorium. He pointed his finger at the stage.

"Do you see that square platform up there?"

"Yes, Fred. That's the stage."

"Yes, the stage. In our business together that's where you will be in charge. You own the stage. In everything else, I will be in charge. Okay?"

I didn't dare protest. Fred was resolving our ongoing battles for control by assigning separate areas of responsibility. I got the areas where I worked best and left him the areas where he had the natural strengths. I got the message. Fred had been doing a good job and needed to be free of my Choleric criticism and Sanguine second-guessing. That didn't mean I couldn't express concerns or tell him what I needed, but when he would then tell me, "I'll take care of it," I had to learn to let go. I had to trust him. And that was the beginning of our harmonious business relationship.

How to Make It Work

Working together as a couple can be exciting and productive if you understand the personalities—or it can lead you toward divorce if you don't. Let's assume you are contemplating a business where you will be working together. Or you may be supervising or working with a married couple and can help them. Here are a few simple steps to keep in mind.

Step 1. Explain what you do like and respect about your mate. Sit down alone together and just listen to each other. Don't interrupt. Thank each other for who he or she is; then repeat the areas you think need to be corrected or at least modified. Listen again. Don't defend yourself. Don't accuse your mate. Conclude by each of you pledging to work on at least one of the problem areas.

Don't use the discussion as ammunition for an attack the next day: "I called three of my friends today and they said you are wrong. I *don't* talk too much," or "I asked the men at work and they say I'm not boring but that you just don't really listen."

You might ask, "What does this have to do with working together?" This is the kindergarten of relationships. If you can't pass this simple test, you'll never get into first grade. Yes, it hurts, but you need to lay these problems out on the table before you enter a business relationship. They won't stay under the carpet for long before one of you is throwing out innuendoes that will trip you both up. At the start of the years I worked with Fred I had no idea how much hostility we had stored up against each other, even though we were polite.

Step 2. Take time to know your inborn personality. If you are still speaking to each other, it is time to review personalities. If you have already done that, go over them again, checking off the strengths and weaknesses you have uncovered together. You'll be thrilled that you're not alone. "All couples have differences, but you are going to embrace the strengths and learn to accept the weaknesses," I told our class. "Each one of you must work prayerfully

151

to overcome these problem areas, even if you don't really believe you have them."

Hans nodded at this and Darlene smiled.

Rose and I have developed this course (and laid out this book) in a format that uses each chapter as one session, so you can develop a plan of teaching others with whom you live or work. You'll be surprised at how all of your differences fit into the personalities. No one needs to be on the defensive. Each personality has value. If you look at your own weaknesses as bad examples, they will become humorous. Fred and I spent twenty years of personality study with amazing results. We called those years the best part of our lives.

Step 3. Be willing to help each other without getting defensive. Don't correct each other in public or make sarcastic allusions. Encourage the other one, notice how much he or she has improved, and thank your mate sincerely. You may be living out a miracle in progress.

Step 4. Set some boundaries for each other as you divide responsibilities. If you can't agree on who takes out the trash or who helps review your child's spelling words at home, you won't be able to work in business together. Fred and I had to set clear personal boundaries. Fred's critique of my speaking the minute I left the stage was *not* good timing, and yet he thought I needed to know so I wouldn't make such mistakes again. I told him I was willing to learn but that he had bad timing. That's when I told him to write down my mistakes on cards and give them to me later—much later—and then I would assimilate the correct information into my material. Eventually he realized it was all Melancholy trivia. None of it made that much difference. I still have the cards he wrote about me, and sometimes I show them to an audience.

Conflict was minimized when we divided up our areas of control. We agreed that what happened on the stage was my area of responsibility. When I walked off the platform, he was in charge. I was the teacher: what I said and did up front was under my direction. He was the manager. When I fell back into the old habit of second-guessing him, he'd say, "Is that an onstage problem?"

I'd think for a second and say, "No."

Then he'd add, "Then I guess you don't have to worry about it." I learned to relax and let go, trust Fred more, and really appreciate his loving protection and direction.

For couples contemplating a business together, remember:

The Sanguine attracts other people and keeps them amused. Don't expect them to explain the finances or plan the schedule. Don't expect them to turn Melancholy to suit you. Let them keep everybody happy and pass out the refreshments.

The Melancholy likes schedules, charts, and graphs and should be the one making them. They can also add columns of figures and tell you when you are spending too much. They can learn to greet people and be charming, but it's not natural or easy. Have them explain the business and reply to questions. They know the answers.

The Choleric doesn't like idle chatter and wants to talk business immediately. They are usually right in their judgment but tend to make others feel insecure. Sometimes they focus more on the project and less on the persons involved. They have a keen business sense and love counting money. Be grateful for their detailed ability and don't make fun of them.

The Phlegmatic is more selective than others about what they get involved in and may not get excited right away, so don't expect immediate support. They will be pleasant and inoffensive, unlike the Choleric. If they see positive results, they will usually pick up their enthusiasm. When they see the value of the task at hand, they'll do the necessary background work without being asked.

Understanding the differences in your personalities will help you and your spouse determine if working at a business together is a good idea. If you decide it is, understanding the personalities will guide you in determining who should take on which responsibilities for the greatest success.

Your Workplace Marriages

These tips are helpful for workplace "marriages" too. Just as people can be "married to their work," people can be "married" to their co-workers when they spend days, weeks, and years together in the same company or industry.

"The interview and hiring process is something like Rose's description of dating and courtship," I told the class. "When you are considering hiring someone, that's the time to take a thorough inventory of their strengths and weaknesses. If you decide to hire them, put them in the right spot where they will shine and then appreciate their contribution. You'll have a happier workplace home!

"If you're the one being hired, try to investigate where you will be working and with whom, and then make your decision. Every workplace relationship will have its ups and downs, strengths and weaknesses. It's up to you to decide on which ones you will focus," I finished.

"I have one more good example of a marriage where the couple worked together," Rose said.

Learning the Fancy Footwork

Matt is Sanguine-Phlegmatic: charming, silly, fun, and personable, with a laid-back but steady approach to business. His wife and business partner, Jen, is a high-energy Choleric-Melancholy combination. How often these exact opposites find each other! Jen has intense drive and the warm, caring sensitivity that is a Melancholy strength, but the stress of the job and her desire for

154

reaching goals can get her so tightly wound up that she sometimes feels she might explode.

"I tend to put too much pressure on myself," she shared. "Then Matt will come along, sit down, and say gently in his soft, Phlegmatic way, 'Let's look at the facts.' He is motivated to do the business, but he refuses to get caught up in all the hype and is much better than I am at setting realistic goals.

"That's why he's so good for me," Jen added. "His calm assurance is like a rock. He keeps me from losing it, and I help him by keeping him on course. Sometimes he gets worn out, too, and I can get him motivated again. But I've also learned that I can't push him. I have to give him the time and space to move when he's ready—but then he really moves! That means I have to let go and trust him. That's hard sometimes."

Matt added, "Yeah, we're really learning how to work with each other in this business. Sometimes we step on each other's toes, but it's like being in a boxing ring. In the first round you think you know what the other guy is going to do, but you really don't until the bell rings and you start working it. You have to learn what his moves are and anticipate them. Then after a few rounds, a lot of sweat—and maybe a few blows—you get a much better feel of whom you're in with."

Jen raised her eyebrows. "Honey, do you mean you see me as your opponent?"

"No!" Matt laughed. "It's a man analogy. You know what I mean, that we are getting to know each other's moves better over time." He gave her his best Sanguine smile. She melted.

"Maybe Matt should have referenced an Arthur Murray dance floor instead of a boxing ring, but since Jen understood Matt's personality, she knew exactly what he meant and didn't take it personally. That's why they are successfully working together," Rose said.

Before we concluded—and to get the group ready for the next class—I asked, "Has anyone ever been approached by a friend or family member who's in multilevel marketing?"

"Yes!" said Fran Taylor. "My sister set me up where I get a lot of my retail purchases online with a company like that and I love it. You get lots of points and prizes. It's fun."

When you are considering hiring someone, that's the time to take a thorough inventory of their strengths and weaknesses.

"Great. I think you'll all appreciate our next session. We have good personality examples from couples who work together specifically in multilevel marketing. But these examples also apply to other industries. And I hope Hans and Darlene will share some of their success tips, too."

"I could probably teach the whole class!" boasted Darlene.

"That's right. She could," said Hans.

"Thanks, everyone," I said. "See you next time!"

What Did We Learn This Time?

- Spouses who work together can benefit from setting boundaries.
- Spouses should focus on the areas where their natural strengths will shine.
- Never berate your spouse in public!
- You can't help your mate unless you respect his/her personality.

11

Personalities in Multilevel Marketing

Hans and Darlene Guttenberg were the first ones to arrive for the class on personalities in multilevel marketing. Hans walked up to the front of the room and said, "Florence, I really appreciate how you describe strengths of the Phlegmatic. We're *not* all couch potatoes." He glanced over at Darlene.

Florence assured Hans that she and I (Rose) both knew that, and we'd come to a deep appreciation of Phlegmatic stability, especially in business.

"You'll enjoy today's stories, Hans," Florence said. "I want both you and Darlene to feel free to share today, especially since you've been in this business for a while. Why don't you go round up those chatty Sanguines out in the hall, and let's get started!"

How It Works

Multilevel or network marketing is an alternative career path that many people ride to riches and others use as a way to increase the family income. Amway is the best-known multilevel marketing company, and Florence has spoken at their conventions at many glamorous resorts in the United States, England, East and West Germany, Hungary, Hong Kong, New Zealand, and many times on her twenty trips to Australia, where she has addressed other multilevel marketing celebrations as well. When the LA Lakers won the 2009 NBA Championship in the Amway Arena in Orlando, it was the founder of Amway who handed Kobe Bryant the trophy.

Multilevel marketing (MLM) is a multibillion-dollar business around the world and offers opportunities to many who never expected to be entrepreneurs. In this type of business—or any business where relationships are key—it's extremely important to understand the personalities.

Perfect for Sanguines

Sanguines love network marketing because it sounds like eternal parties and conventions. The women can wear sequin-laden gowns and the men tuxedos. Sanguines are the best at conversing with strangers, daring to invite them to a meeting, and shining up front as they give their business testimony.

Sanguines love network marketing because it sounds like eternal parties and conventions.

The Sanguine wit and charm can easily captivate others, and their love of talking on the phone helps them motivate those who work for them (their down-line). Their life seems to be one big celebration, and they draw people to them. The best place for the Sanguine is in these social situations.

Their weakness is their lack of innate business sense. They love money and will work hard to earn it, but they are far better at spending it than adding up all those columns and getting it to the bank. The Sanguine needs a Melancholy partner who will handle the finances with ease. But there will likely be a big weakness in this combination: the Sanguine will make mistakes and the Melancholy partner will take sadistic pleasure at pointing out these errors to the whole group, thus humiliating the Sanguine, who will then want to quit.

A Great Opportunity

"Rose, why don't you come up and share your multilevel story with our group?" Florence asked.

"Thought you'd never ask," I said as I got up quickly to take over from her.

"*You've* been in network marketing?" asked Darlene. She seemed surprised.

"Oh-h-h-h, yeah . . ." I drawled. "It's a great business, but not knowing the personalities can really limit people's potential. I'd love to talk with you and Hans after class is over, okay?"

"That would be nice, thanks," said Darlene. Hans nodded in agreement.

"As a Sanguine-Choleric, I couldn't *wait* to get into multilevel marketing," I began. "At first, I knew very little about the concept, but friends had invited us over for a lovely dinner and my husband—who sad to say has been my ex for some time now—and I were happy to spend time with them. After a decadent dessert and hot coffee, they shared about a new business they'd joined and said they were hoping we'd consider coming aboard too."

I was attracted by the promises of luxury homes and fat retirement accounts, and I also loved the thought of fun trips, joining a wide circle of new friends we'd make, giant rallies held in cities around the country, and corporate events that were more like big block parties. And no matter the personality, I think most women love the thought of working with their husband in a business where they share common goals and dreams.

My Phlegmatic husband was quickly drawn to the idea of making lots of money "the easy way." As our friends showed us colored brochures of magnificent mansions and sleek racing boats, I could see his eyes widen. He wasn't jumping out of his seat—yet—because his Melancholy side was prudently wary, but eventually the "easy" part won out. The deal was cinched when he could see that I was excited about it and he would not have to do this all alone. That night we signed up.

As a Choleric, I love to get started on any new project, so the next day I ran right out and bought twenty-four bright yellow folders with coordinating sticky labels. Into my shopping basket I also threw a red plastic carrying case for the folders and a pack of colored pens. I came home with bags full of home office accessories and began to get ready for the new business. I hadn't yet thought of how I would organize it all, but that would come later. It didn't matter, for I was in Sanguine-Choleric heaven!

Charting a Course

"Let's talk about charts for a minute," I said. "I can easily create charts and graphs and categorize things, not because I am a perfect Melancholy, but because as a Choleric I crave order and enjoy multitasking. Charts let a Choleric see just how much work she is accomplishing!"

The differences between a Choleric chart and a Melancholy chart are speed and perfection. Cholerics put them together quickly—maybe drawn by hand—and with just enough order so they can get moving. But Melancholies might spend hours redoing the charts or making alternate charts in different fonts—or going to the internet to find a program that allows you to make multiple charts at once. Sigh! By that time the Choleric has made the chart, filled it in, done the tasks, and moved on to another chore.

Phlegmatic charts are often the most carefully planned, but they tend to stay in the person's head. The perfect, peaceful time to devote to the chart can't be planned; it just has to happen, but it rarely does. Sometimes Phlegmatics realize they need a time chart to plan to make the other charts, but then they just get too overwhelmed and give up.

Sanguine charts look good but may be missing a day or week or an important column. They hang brightly in the office workspace but are often forgotten or lost.

While the Sanguines like colored folders and pens, Melancholies are most happy with manila folders and black pens. "That's how *real* businesses do it!" While the Sanguines love an assortment of pens (at least the ones they haven't lost), the Melancholies have one or two expensive ones and take pride in using them. While Sanguines like decorations on their desk (plants, figurines, and dusty trophies), the Melancholy likes the sleek look, not an extra, unnecessary paper or paperclip in view—unless they are the extra-creative type who gets deeply lost in their work and are too focused to clean the desk.

Having learned from my earlier and more chaotic days that Sanguines are not naturally orderly or perfectionists, I'd allowed my Choleric side to take charge with a well-ordered life. As long as I could still have fun at it, I'd be fine. So after hearing about how to get started in the multilevel marketing business, I made all the files our friends told us we needed. Then all I had to do was wait for my husband to jump in too.

Taking the Lead

Our first assignment was to make lists of all our friends, family members, people we knew at church, casual acquaintances, and store clerks with whom we were friendly. Our goal was to share the business plan with them while we were being mentored by our friends and their up-line—those ahead of us in the business structure. I made my list and my husband made his. But for all his strengths and kind heart, my Phlegmatic husband was not the leader in our marriage or in this new business because I'd assumed the role of major decision maker. Not that I didn't want him to take

161

charge, but he often hesitated—and all that did was automatically draw me into the leadership position. But now, with this new business venture, I was trying hard not to be the boss and to create a space for him to take charge. Our contact lists were finished, but weeks went by and nothing got done.

Our mentor friends called and encouraged us, and I hoped their pep talk would motivate my husband. They even came over one night to light a fire under us. I was ready, but I was trying very carefully to allow my husband the time and space to move at his pace and in his way. We'd been learning about the personalities and I knew that I had a Choleric tendency to take charge whenever he didn't move quickly enough for me. He was smart in lots of areas and motivated in some, but we'd fallen into the pattern of my doing the planning and implementing almost everything in our life, from the budget to vacations to where we would have dinner. He'd provide loving support but little leadership, and I was tired of that.

When we argued, I would give logical reasons why something should be done, and he would just tune me out. We didn't yell or scream, but we were like two foreigners trying to get the other one to hear, because *we didn't speak each other's personality language*. Eventually we had a long, honest talk and decided not to do the business; I didn't want to run the show anymore, and he realized he was happy with his job as a firefighter, where he could sit at the station all day with a few fellow firemen watching television and waiting for emergency calls. My Phlegmatic husband was excellent in emergencies—staying calm, working hard to fight fires, and saving lives—but was happy to return to nap, polish the fire engine, and wait for another catastrophe.

"There were lots of reasons we ended up divorcing, and I'll be the first to admit my own fault," I said. "But a big part of it was that from the beginning we didn't know ourselves or who the other was, and we kept trying to change each other. This happens in marriages and at work."

Hans and Darlene exchanged a knowing look. Was I imagining it, or were they softening toward each other? I hoped they were.

"If you're a Choleric who wants to go into business with or marry a Phlegmatic, it's important that you both know ahead of time exactly what will be required of you and that the Phlegmatic be given reasonable time to think about it and decide if they want to do it or not," I said. "There's no doubt Phlegmatics can work hard and provide strong support *if that's what they have chosen to do*. Most of them, however, will probably follow a partner into the business before they have given it enough thought and then decide midstream it is not for them. The Cholerics need to respect that decision but be smart enough to help them make it much earlier."

I wanted to end on a lighter note, so I said, "If I had known all this back then, I could have saved the cost of all those colored folders!" The Sanguines laughed.

How the Personalities Help

Even though the customer might not always be right, it's always the right thing to recognize their personality as quickly as possible. Louisa has relied on the personalities to help equip her network marketing sales force to be successful. She shared: "We use the personalities in workshops to equip people for their work with customers and co-workers. We challenge them to think about these questions and then answer them."

> *Even though the customer might not always be right, it's always the right thing to recognize their personality as quickly as possible.*

Can you think of something that really annoys you about your spouse or a client? Identify what personality style might be behind it.

How do you get an extremely Choleric person to try a new product?

How can you package an offer in an easy way to interest a Phlegmatic?

How can you help a Sanguine stay focused on a goal for the whole month?

How can you help a Melancholy stop ruminating and start moving?

Louisa reports that one of the more fun training exercises is to role-play, with everyone getting to act out—and exaggerate for effect—their opposite personalities. "We have so much fun and we see results every day! Knowing the personalities has increased our bottom line."

Florence and I recently had lunch with her friend Pat, who is also in multilevel marketing. She arrived with her bright makeup, sweeping eyelashes, and sparkling sequins on her dress—with shoes to match. She didn't have to tell me her personality, but she did.

"I'm Sanguine—outgoing and enthusiastic—and I love everyone I meet; in fact, I don't think I've ever met anyone who I thought was a stranger," Pat admitted. "It's possible that some of these people have not found me totally charming at all times, but actually I've been so enthralled in my attempts to enthrall them that I really haven't noticed!"

Does that sound familiar to any of you Melancholies?

"It never occurred to me," Pat continued, "that anyone would want actual facts in lieu of my very animated and entertaining presentation of the fun we would be having together in the future. Occasionally—since I represent a line of health and beauty products—the questions would become somewhat technical. Not having the exact data that they wanted, my normal reply would be something like: 'If the vitamins don't keep you alive, the beauty products will make you look great at the end!' I know some don't think that's too funny, but I do!"

In the beginning of her career, Pat figured that those who didn't want to skip with her down the yellow brick road of life were somehow deficient. It didn't occur to her that they had different temperaments—and therefore different emotional needs, which, when satisfied, would help them want to come on board with the business.

"After I read *Personality Plus*—a few times—I finally understood that everyone plays an important role, seeks a different answer, and deserves a patient mentor in their life. Sanguines aren't naturally patient, but with a mature attitude they can learn to give others what they need. I've made many mistakes, but over the years I've made great strides in recognizing, relating to, and enjoying all of the personalities."

Today Pat relies on her natural charm, her sweet attitude toward others, her ability to carry on conversations, and her tendency to lighten up a room with her funny and encouraging stories. After Pat started her business thirty-five years ago, her mother told her, "Thank goodness, Pat. You've finally found something where you're being paid for your mouth."

We All Want to Be Nice

Sometimes the worst thing a person can be is "nice." In our politically correct culture, niceness has run amok. We are afraid to offend anyone about anything, and if we do, we may even face a lawsuit for hurting someone's feelings.

I met Charlotte at a convention, and she shared that in her networking organization there is a real problem with ineffective speakers and their tortured audiences. Charlotte is an impatient Choleric, and what she observed is important to multilevel marketing organizations as well as traditional businesses that hold conferences and motivational meetings. "Just because someone has been successful doesn't make them a good speaker. Many of them don't plan their talks. They ramble or rant—depending on their personality—and sometimes they even cry. All that does is turn off anyone who is listening: the Cholerics get irritated, the Phlegmatics fall asleep, the Sanguines start looking around or talking to their neighbor, and the Melancholies get quietly disgusted and depressed."

Charlotte also pinpointed the reason her company allows these disastrous meetings to keep occurring. "We all want to be nice. No one wants to say, 'No, your ideas are totally absurd. All you do is wander in your thoughts, and everyone is sick of your tears.' People tend to think that's mean, and it sure isn't nice. Everyone is afraid to speak the truth in a loving manner, even our managers."

Charlotte went on. "A prudent leader must have the courage to protect the audience first, even if it means talking with the speaker about her message. Ask the speaker to plan her talk, give you an outline, and practice it before delivering it. Make sure you give her a time limit, and if she goes over, move up next to her and quickly thank her when she takes her next big breath."

If the speaker can't—or won't—comply, an effective leader must kindly but firmly make the decision to get another speaker or hire a professional to train local speakers. The leader owes that to the company. Everyone loves to tell their "story," but not everyone wants or needs to hear it.

Phlegmatics have observed life and have a lot to say but often are not skilled at opening up and sharing effectively. They need structure (a clear point and an outline) and a time limit. Most Phlegmatics need to be encouraged to pick up the pace, get to the point, and make sure there is a "flavor" to their talk besides vanilla!

Giving an effective talk can prove difficult for the other personalities as well:

> *Sanguines* will capture the audience immediately, but will they hold on to them? Sanguines are quick to be transparent with an audience, but they can become too emotionally "naked." They also need structure and a time limit. Caution them not to get off on a tangent of funny stories.

166

Cholerics can present a commanding presence, but often their talk turns into a long list of commands or a recitation of their successes. Help them soften the message—if necessary—and instead of speaking as a detached instructor, help them connect personally with the audience. Transparency is key for a Choleric.

Melancholies can bring a sincere heart and real depth to a talk, but they sometimes go too far, giving far more details than are really necessary. Remind them that the talk should not be just about the problems but should offer clear and uplifting solutions. Handouts of the outline and statistics will save time.

Workable for All

There's room for every personality in multilevel marketing, but it's important as you build your business to understand the personalities and how each personality can be successful—and how the business can work for each one. There's no way that all men are born leaders and all women passive followers.

Our next chart points out the different approaches that should be taken when trying to attract a Sanguine, Choleric, Phlegmatic, or Melancholy to multilevel marketing. "For each one a different approach should be taken to make contact, present the plan, follow up, help the person build business, and give guidance," I said.

After class, I wasn't surprised when the Guttenbergs approached me, and Darlene spoke first. "Rose, I really appreciate your sharing your personal story today. You could have been talking about me and Hans."

"Yes, but I have much more motivation than your ex-husband," said Hans.

Darlene agreed. "You do, Hans. And I guess we both need to start appreciating each other more." She knew how to say the right thing, but I knew—from my own experience—it was probably very difficult for her to live it.

I asked her, "Darlene, do you get scared that you're really all alone in this endeavor and nothing will ever get done if you're not there to take care of it?"

"Yes! All the time!" Her hard demeanor softened a little.

"Hans, *is* she alone?" I asked directly.

He was quick to reply. "No, I love this business. I do. And I want to be the rock that Darlene needs."

"I know you do, Hans. I could tell from the first day you two walked in our classroom."

I decided to give them the two-minute pep talk that I often give myself when I (the pushy Choleric) am working with any Phlegmatic. I moved in close to them both so no one else could hear, and I reached for Darlene's arm.

"Give Hans some time and space to do what he needs to do. Make sure you've really clarified the details for him. Set a reasonable deadline and be willing to extend it a bit if he needs. Ask him directly what you can do to help, or not. Don't assume. Then trust him, despite his past failures. You have to let go a little. Maybe a lot."

Then I looked over at Hans. "Yes, past failures, Hans!" I gave a little laugh to soften his sensitive side without being mocking. "We all make them. Let's just keep learning from them. You've got to show Darlene she can lean on you. Instead of resenting her pushiness and shutting down, why don't you sit *her* down, ask for some negotiating time, and work through the problem? You are a natural problem solver. I know you can do it!"

I looked back and forth at each of them. "Okay?"

I didn't want to become their marriage counselor, but I did want to call them to a higher level of working with and appreciating each other.

They both smiled and nodded. As I drew away, he put his arm around her and pulled her in close.

She let him . . . and that's progress.

What Did We Learn This Time?

This time we have a handy reference chart to help you!

Building the Business in Multilevel Marketing

Popular Sanguine	Powerful Choleric
Making contact • ask about her family or friends to establish rapport • ask about her schedule to determine feasibility	*Making contact* • ask about his line of work and job stability • ask about his goals, where he wants to be in two to five years
Presenting the plan • build dreams • focus on social aspects of the business and recognition • avoid too many details • use her name and the names of friends frequently	*Presenting the plan* • focus on the process of building a team • stick to the bottom line • point out his leadership strengths • offer him control of his financial future
Following up • use social chitchat • ask questions about her and her dreams • praise her people skills • encourage her to make a list of friends • emphasize the excitement of a new adventure	*Following up* • plan a specific timeline and offer a meeting overview • be businesslike and professional • stress the importance of a tried-and-true plan for success • focus on his control of his future
Building the business • help her define, set, and commit to goals • be sure she has accurate information on her leads list	*Building the business* • get goals and completion dates on paper • help him think through potential leads • remind him that the business is based on numbers of contacts • encourage him to follow the system
Guidance • offer guidance on business skills • meet over coffee or for lunch to talk • show her how to have fun while building the business • offer to help with follow-up • remind her that books and tapes will help her help others	*Guidance* • focus on the process to financial freedom • remind him that he has control of when he increases income and when he gets "promoted" • emphasize the need to follow the duplication process

Peaceful Phlegmatic	Perfect Melancholy
Making contact • ask about family or recreational activities • help him identify what is really important; is there someone special he would like to help?	*Making contact* • ask about her job, organization, and how she prioritizes tasks • share a proven pattern for success that is organized and can be duplicated
Presenting the plan • emphasize that working now can mean an early retirement • ask many questions to be sure he understands • work with him to identify his primary dream • show how patience and ability to get along with others will help him	*Presenting the plan* • stress importance of organization and sensitivity • discover an area where more money or time would help make her life more perfect • be sure all your math is correct • share stories of others in similar places who have done it
Following up • realize he may be difficult to read • tell him of others who are now retired, enjoying the fruits of their labor • keep the meeting short • guide him in his goals	*Following up* • be ready for her questions • offer proof of security and income potential • substantiate claims • share profiles of leadership
Building the business • encourage him to listen for people's dreams • remind him of the value of this opportunity for others	*Building the business* • review her goals and see if they can be sped up • encourage her to make her lists and actually call the people • remind her of her dream of financial security
Guidance • initiate the session • push him to be the leader of his group	*Guidance* • as a private person, she needs to be encouraged to share struggles • may become depressed if business is not moving at desired pace • focus on what she is doing correctly • be generous with tips for movement

12

Personalities in Real Estate

"Rose will be teaching this session since she's been in real estate most of her life," Florence told our group. "Today I'll be the one in the back of the room just listening." Our students enjoyed hearing us tease each other.

"Fine with me," I (Rose) replied. "And when I want some coffee, will you be humble enough to go get me a cup?"

Florence thought, and then added wistfully, "Where is Fred when we need him?"

"Yes! Fred!" I looked out at the class and told them, "Fred would have gotten us *all* coffee—and donuts to go with it! He was such a strong, servant-hearted man." It had been several years since he died, and all of us who were blessed to know him still missed him. The moment was almost melancholy.

Yes, Sanguines can appreciate "melancholy." We just don't want to stay there too long. So I called the class to order and began our session on the personalities who work in real estate.

"Most of you—as intelligent as I know you all are—have a pretty strong grasp on the four personalities by now. While we share today's stories about personalities in real estate–related offices, I want you to pay attention to a central theme of selfishness. Florence and I have discovered that a self-serving attitude is really at the root of most of the personality problems in the workplace, or anywhere else for that matter."

"Rose, you are so right," Darlene interjected. "Now that we understand the personalities, Hans and I have been talking about our own children and when their little personalities became problems. It was always when they were afraid they wouldn't get their own way. It was selfishness, alright! Our Melancholy daughter went into sulky moods and our Choleric son would throw screaming tantrums."

"Thanks, Darlene. Each personality has its natural strengths, but when *fear* and *selfishness* set in, those strengths become disordered and carried to an extreme and become weaknesses. And remember, in our workplaces we might have those same little children running around in grown-up bodies. Let me start by sharing a time I wasn't the most mature I could have been."

Selfishness Distorts Strengths

The following story is a perfect example of what happens when unchecked emotions take over. The extroverted Choleric will want to rise up and smash others down. If they have a little Melancholy in them, they'll also take delight afterward in grinding their opponents into little piles of dust. The extroverted Sanguines may scream and yell, but they still want you to love them; after their tirade, they usually burst into tears—and want that healing hug.

And the introverted Melancholies and Phlegmatics? They'll run for the hills—or the break room—hide behind anything (or anyone), and point their fingers accusingly at the monstrous, out-of-control maniacs who are trying to take over the world.

"I had a commercial real estate appraisal assignment to complete and the deadline was fast approaching," I began. "The property owner, the project lender, and a long list of other involved people were waiting for my report so they could close a several-million-dollar financing deal on an upscale condo project in Palm Springs. The pressure was on. Knowing at the onset what would be needed to complete my work, I'd contacted the architect's office for a full set of project blueprints well in advance. I phoned, identified the project, left my name and telephone number, and told the man who answered what I needed. He assured me someone would get back to me. Of course, no one did."

To make sure I was covered I'd also sent an email to the company. Even though I'm Sanguine, I've had to learn over the years that if I don't get organized, write it all down, follow up, and keep notes, I'll be in big trouble. And as a Choleric, I never want anyone coming back to me to point out my mistakes!

More than a week went by and I received no word. The client had called to pressure me. *Where is my appraisal?* I'd proceeded as far as I could and now I had to have those plans! So my assistant and I got in the car and drove thirty minutes to Palm Springs to the architect's office. No one was there at the front entry to greet us, so we walked through a maze of cubicles and came to the far back room. There sat a quiet Melancholy-Phlegmatic architect who showed almost no emotion when we walked directly into his workspace.

How do I know what his personality was? Architects tend to be creative, imaginative Melancholy planners; they also work with precise angles and square feet and geometric formulas that would make a Sanguine's head spin. And the draftsmen (or women) have to have great Phlegmatic patience to sit at their tilted worktables and make every single little measurement add up perfectly. If they don't, the buildings in every city would be collapsing around us.

"Hi, I'm Rose Sweet, and I called last week on the condo project and the plans I need," I said and smiled and batted my eyes as I always do to disarm anyone who might get irritated that I am making demands. He acted as though he had never heard of me. Maybe he hadn't. I didn't know who he was, and he didn't disclose his identity. His face was blank, but he could see from my pent-up energy that he'd better at least write my name down and pretend that he cared about helping me.

"Everyone is out, but I'll take down your number."

I came closer and stood next to him as he slowly took a notepad from the cluttered papers on his desk. It was messy, but Melancholies can keep all that organized in their heads. As I surveyed the piles on his desk, I saw a large note right next to his phone that read, "Rose Sweet needs plans for project. Please call [phone number] and get her what she needs right away."

It was dated weeks ago, when I had first called. I couldn't believe it! Clearly someone had given him the message, and he'd just let it sit there the whole time. It's not only Cholerics who hate to admit they are wrong—*everyone does*. It's just that the extroverts (Cholerics and Sanguines) are often the first to vocalize their innocence. The introverts usually sit quietly and say nothing, hoping no one will notice their mistakes. If someone does, even an introvert can find a voice in coming up with excuses, or they might just remain silent.

"Hey! *That's me!*" I smiled again. "See? . . . here's the note when I called *weeks ago*. See?" I picked up the pad and practically shoved it in his face, still with a (controlling) Sanguine smile. I expected him to react in humble apologies, offer to run and get my plans, copy them, and hand them to me—right here, right now. But he didn't. He didn't show any emotion whatsoever.

"Well, I'll call you when we can get them to you," he said.

I thought, *That's it?* He was not going to make any extra effort, and since I knew personalities, I knew that if I pushed any harder, he'd resist even more. Sadly, I saw that my delightful smile and sweet charm hadn't had any effect on him either. I decided I'd have to take another approach. I'd go back to my office and call his boss.

174

I took a deep breath and tried to smile. "I need them today, *please*. My client is waiting. Thank you." We left and drove back to the office.

I called his boss and asked for her help. It worked. Later that afternoon he sent me an email with the plans attached as a pdf file and included a short note of transmittal: "I hope these help and I hope you can have a spa day in the near future. You seem very stressed."

Argh-h-h! How dare he suggest a spa day? I wanted to throttle him. *Did he even have an idea of the pressure I was under? Stressed? I was nice in his office . . . he should see stressed! Why, he doesn't even know me!* I know that's not very nice, but that's how angry Cholerics think (and sometimes talk) when they're reacting and *not* thinking!

My Melancholy-Phlegmatic mother had done this to me all my life: whenever I—as a high-energy Sanguine-Choleric—would get ruffled and begin to demonstrate visible anxiety, she would immediately go into super-slow, almost comatose mode as a contrast to show how calm *she* was and how out of control I was. This is a common pattern between introverts and extroverts, and it infuriates the Choleric even more. Phlegmatics know it. That's how they gain control.

But no matter how upset someone is, or how emotional he or she has become, this response is not very loving, and it's a smug way to point fingers instead of meeting needs.

I got the plans, finished the job, and my client was happy.

And you can be sure I waited at least six months before making an appointment for a spa day. Then it seemed like it was my idea.

How to Handle the "Looky-Loos"

Holly raised her hand. "Rose, may I share my observations about problem people? I run into them all the time when I am trying to sell homes."

"Yes, Holly. I was about to ask if you had any good real estate–related stories. Please, go ahead."

Holly told of having to show properties to different potential home buyers, and how the four personalities invariably made a difference in how the meetings went.

"The Cholerics are great at making up their minds quickly and getting right to the point. They ask the right questions and they don't play games. But . . . since the real estate market has dropped dramatically in the last few years, some of them think they can buy a home for practically nothing. They make ridiculously low bids and then outwardly scoff when the seller rejects their offer. When it becomes clear that the seller won't budge, they usually pull out intimidation tactics, like *I guess you don't really want to make a commission, do you?* At first it made me want to burst into tears, but then I realized they were trying to control me. I have enough Choleric in me that I can stand up to it. I just had to remember it wasn't about me; it was about the Choleric pushing hard to get what they want."

Holly smiled. "The Sanguines are great. They love every property and can see themselves decorating each home we visit. The male Sanguines like to plan party patios and big backyards. But I have to make sure they are qualified for a home loan first, because despite their happy countenances, they often have crummy credit!

"The Melancholies usually have the highest credit scores and always show up on time for the appointment. I like that. And they turn in their paperwork promptly and perfectly. But—and this is a big but—they are the worst when it comes to inspection time." Holly groaned and rolled her eyes dramatically. "*The worst!* My charm never works on them! They want to know about the roof, the air-conditioning, the plumbing, and of course termites. If they see a scratch or a missing tile they want the whole house redone before they will close escrow. They want tornado, hurricane, and earthquake protection because they just know something bad will happen once they move in. I've just learned to expect it and be ready for them, because they will not sign those papers until everything is perfect! I really earn my commissions on those!"

Dr. Hastings threw his head back and laughed out loud, as though Holly's tale of woe had reminded him of something—his own home buying experience, perhaps? For those of us who were used to his dignified demeanor, it was a rare moment.

"Finally there are the Phlegmatics." Holly paused. "I wonder why we always list them last? I guess it's because the others can be so . . . dramatic! Oh well. They are so nice. They never really get upset at anything. But they can never make up their mind! Usually they have an outgoing spouse who is excited about the perfect house that seems to meet all their requirements, but the Phlegmatic will quietly say, 'Let's look at a few others before we make up our minds,' or 'What about that one on Elm Street that you really liked?' Once you know them, these personalities are all so predictable!"

"Holly, great insight," I said. "You should hold a seminar for the board of realtors in your area! Why don't you come up to the whiteboard right now and write down four tips you'd give to others in real estate to meet the emotional needs of these four types of home buyers."

Without hesitation, Holly jumped up and grabbed the marker. Here is what she wrote:

Cholerics—Let them bluster. Don't get sucked into their pushy ways, but don't take any abuse, either.

Sanguines—Have your Melancholy assistant make sure the Sanguines are prequalified. Then just enjoy your time with them.

Melancholies—Do your homework and make sure there are no problems with the property, or the Melancholy will make you pull all kinds of clearance reports.

Phlegmatics—Limit the number of properties you might be willing to show the Phlegmatics. They have lots of time and will want to look at them all. It takes them forever to make up their minds.

Everyone smiled, and I moved back in charge of the class.

"I have another story that I think you'll all enjoy. Choleric Jim runs a high-powered real estate investment group in northern California, where flipping single-family homes has been generating considerable income."

"What is flipping?" asked Fran. "I know it in skirts, but not in real estate."

I explained that flipping has become the common term for purchasing and fixing a property that needs a little work, adding a few cosmetic touches, and selling it again within a few months for a higher price. Then I told how I talked to Bob, the company's advertising and marketing consultant.

"Flipped!" Bob said. "Perfect word, Rose. The houses aren't the only ones that get flipped out in this place. This office can drive me crazy!" Bob's a thoughtful Melancholy—he likes things done intentionally and well. He's also Phlegmatic, the calm personality that can bring strong support to any workplace. He told me he has had to learn to deal with Jim's Choleric intensity.

"When I first heard you speak on the personalities and heard the description of Choleric, I thought, *That's Jim*! He has constant high energy, all right—which is great for selling—but imagine our office as a big kitchen: Jim runs in, rattles the pots and pans around, fills them up, fires up all the burners, gets things 'cooking,' then leaves the room. Someone has to follow him around and make sure things don't boil over or burn up. That's me. I guess because of my Phlegmatic personality it comes naturally."

By understanding the personalities, Bob sees that every Choleric—and the company in which they work—can benefit from a supportive and balanced Phlegmatic. Bob summed it up quite simply, "You could say that Jim picks up properties . . . and I pick up the pieces."

178

Darlene noticeably shifted in her chair and looked over at her Phlegmatic husband, Hans. "Honey, I hate to admit it but I see myself in that kitchen scenario." Now everyone in the room was listening, but Darlene continued anyway. Hans was quiet.

"I never really stopped to think about how much you do for me in our business. I guess I need to thank you for being the one who picks up *my* pieces!" She leaned over and kissed him lightly on his reddened cheek. No one said a word; Hans just smiled.

Just then there was a knock at the classroom door, but I knew who it was. I went over and let my sister Malia into the room.

"Everyone, may I introduce my sister Malia to you. She's in real estate, and I invited her to drive out today and talk with you. She's been very successful in using the knowledge of personalities in her business, and I thought you might like to hear from someone other than me today."

"Thanks, Rose," said Malia. "Someone much younger than you, too, right?" She smiled brightly at the class and told them that I was, indeed, her *much* older sister.

I ignored her comment as I always do. "Malia, I love your story of Alice, and I know the class would appreciate it. Why don't you start with that? The floor is all yours."

But as I walked to the back of the room to take a seat, I told the class, "I may *be* older, but I *look* younger!" I hated to give up the stage without a good laugh.

Malia began, "I've worked in the Palms Springs area in the title insurance business for over thirty years. As a Choleric-Melancholy, I wanted to have the most effective office team who did things perfectly, so I began a study of the personalities. Sanguines and Phlegmatics always perplexed me, until I understood their strengths. One of my dearest friends in the business—Alice—was a Sanguine real estate agent.

"She was always the most beautiful and best-dressed woman of all the local realtors. She was sweet, sassy, and full of sparkle. Before the internet, realtors would invest in mass-mailing campaigns, sending out marketing postcards to potential residential and commercial customers. Alice would hire me to produce and mail her cards. But she didn't do the typical business cards." Malia grinned.

"Her cards were hilarious," she explained. "They had nothing to do with real estate and everything to do with Alice. Once Alice had me scan a picture of the Mona Lisa and superimpose a tennis racquet in her hand. That card was the talk of the town. Alice was the reigning champion at the Indian Wells tennis club that year and wanted everyone to remember it.

"Another time when we had the annual Bob Hope Golf Classic tournament—and all four living presidents of the United States (Carter, Bush Sr., Ford, and Reagan) played golf together—Alice had me take their picture at the first tee and cut and paste her into it. That postcard read, 'It's not what you know, it's who you know!'"

"Alice was fashionable, flashy, and had a way of charming others to do her work. She'd take off every summer for three months when the average daytime desert temperatures rose to about 110 degrees. But in September she'd return to work and be in a complete panic. 'Malia, I need to meet with you,' she'd say. 'Immediately! I just don't know what I'm going to do! I have no business. How am I going to make any money?'

"I suggested that maybe she shouldn't run off and play every summer. 'Oh no, not that. I know what to do. I'll say lots of Hail Mary's. I'll ask God to bring me some business.'"

Malia explained to the class, "Alice was a devout Catholic and relied on her prayers to get her through the tough times. She truly was a good Christian woman who cared about all her clients and friends in the business. One of the ways she kept her business going was that she was completely honest with everyone. She lived her faith on a day-to-day basis.

"Her post-vacation panic happened every year for over ten years, until finally when I got her call in September I stopped trying to figure out a plan for her. I'd simply ask, 'Alice, have you said your Hail Mary's?' No matter what course of advertising and promotion action I suggested, all Alice was willing to do was say those prayers . . . and then expect me and everyone else she knew to help her build her business back up. And the funny thing is that we were all happy to do it for her. It was just like Tom Sawyer and the whitewashed picket fence. Guess what would always happen? After those prayers—and some clever ad work from us—Alice would sell a million-dollar home when no one else was selling anything. God always heard her prayers."

Malia added that Alice had a heart of gold. "One year I was out of the office after surgery to have my gall bladder removed. I had four young children at home, and Alice was one of the few people in our field who remembered to call and see how I was doing. I told her I was nauseated, couldn't move, and had jaundice. 'Oh my goodness!' Alice replied. 'When I had my gall bladder out, I was on the tennis courts two days later!'

"I just ignored the comment and thanked Alice for her call. A day or so later there was a knock on my front door. It was a professional caterer whose arms were full with covered plates of food. 'Hello. I've been engaged to provide you with dinner, and if I can get someone to help me I have more dishes out in my truck,' she said, much to my surprise. Alice had hired the catering company to bring enough meals for me and my family for the next week. Even though it frustrated us how easily she could charm us all into doing her work for her, she had the biggest Sanguine heart and would do anything to make you happy."

Carmen nodded. "Our junior high history teacher does the same thing. You just can't get mad at her," she added. Then she asked, "What's Alice doing now?"

"Alice passed away last April, but she didn't just die. She went out with a Sanguine flair—at sunrise on Easter morning. At her funeral I shared the story of how she sent the caterer and so many more fun and loving things she did. Everyone loved Alice and remembered how she made us do all the hard work while she just looked pretty and made commissions. Now, none of us in real estate in the desert will ever go through Easter without remembering Sanguine Alice."

It was the perfect story to end a day's session that had started with selfishness. With a generous heart, every personality is able to work in their strengths and no one will mind their weaknesses. Florence and I thanked Malia for coming, and I invited the class to join my sister and me afterward for coffee.

"And speaking about generous hearts," added Florence, "I'm asking you all to pray for me and my daughter Marita and our trip to Montreal this week where we will be speaking to three thousand business leaders on *Personality Plus*."

"Oh my!" said Carmen. "That would be a pretty large classroom, wouldn't it?" Everyone could tell that Carmen seemed overwhelmed at the thought.

Pastor Paul piped up. "Florence, of course we'll pray for you. What specifically should we be praying about?"

Florence continued, "We've learned that 90 percent of the audience speaks only French, and so we will be simultaneously translated. This puts an additional burden on the speaker."

Holly Homes told Florence, "Well, we know you'll be just fine. You have the perfect personality for that!" Everyone laughed.

Before the group filed out of our classroom, Florence gave them an assignment.

"Our topic next week will be on personalities in the area of food service. Marita and I will be paying special attention on this trip to all the restaurant personnel we interact with and ask that you do the same this weekend. Wherever you go to eat, take note of the people: those waiting on you, the hostess, and the other diners. And next week we'll find out what *you* found out! Bon appétit!"

What Did We Learn This Time?

- Fear and selfishness will bring out personality weaknesses.
- Kindness and generosity will bring out personality strengths.
- Let the Cholerics bluster and don't overreact to them.
- Make sure the Sanguines are prequalified for financing.
- Do your homework for the Melancholy.
- Help the Phlegmatic by narrowing their many choices.

13

Personalities in Food Services

When we returned for our next class session, Rose and I (Florence) both had wonderful illustrations about our recent restaurant experiences. We planned to begin the session with our stories and then invite the group to tell theirs. I was excited to share about the trip Marita and I had just experienced in Canada, and as soon as the class was settled, I began.

"What an amazing weekend Marita and I had in Quebec! We were grateful to stay in a hotel with a high-class restaurant, and we enjoyed observing the personalities while we dined. Before we ask for your examples, let me share our story."

Because we had arrived at midnight the evening before, we had slept late and arrived downstairs almost at noon. We took a broad look at the restaurant and saw that it was divided into two areas. On one side there was a delightful bright and sunny section by the windows, facing the sidewalk full of people racing to get lunch. On the other side was a dark area with no windows and several families with boisterous young children. It took us two Cholerics no time to decide where we wanted to sit. We were pleasant and in no hurry and saw only a few people sitting on the sunny side.

No one was at the reception desk, so we just waited patiently as the sign requested. When the hostess finally appeared, she walked slowly and didn't seem to notice us. Marita said, "Good morning!" in English, and the girl looked startled. As she tilted her head up we saw big brown eyes, no makeup, and mousy, beige-toned hair. She asked, "Did you want to eat?" We nodded yes, and I mentioned that we would like to sit over by the window.

"That part is closed," she answered. Now you know that when two Cholerics are told they can't sit at one of thirty empty tables, they won't accept defeat easily.

"There are people at two tables!" Marita explained. "We'd like one of those empty ones by the window."

"Those people are just leftovers from before we closed down," the hostess said sadly.

"Could you just pretend *we* are leftovers?" I asked.

"No, I just follow the rules." She looked back down at her paperwork and left us to think about it.

Soon the manager appeared before us. Striding toward us with fists clenched, she asked, "What seems to be the trouble here?"

The Phlegmatic hostess explained, "These people won't sit where I told them to. They want a table by the window." We were immediately the "bad guys."

"She's right. You can't sit there. We've already closed off that section."

At that point the families in the dark section where she wanted us to sit began gathering their things and preparing to leave. As they filed past us, the manager got exasperated and said, "Sit wherever you want." She pushed the hesitant hostess aside and began to cash out the family group. Marita and I moved out of the way and proceeded to the windows. The best tables had not yet been bussed, but that's no problem for two people who've been in the restaurant business for twenty years. My husband, Fred, and I had owned Good Time Charlie's when the children were young, and our whole family had been involved in operating restaurants.

We piled the dishes onto the other cluttered table, brushed the crumbs off the surface with a used napkin, and started to sit down when the waiter appeared wearing a name tag that read "Pierre."

"You can't do that," he said, with a worried look.

"Do what?" Marita asked as we plunked down on the green leather chairs.

"You can't bus tables. That's the busboy's job."

Marita added, "Well, he didn't show up so we did it. We don't mind."

He was obviously a rule-abiding Melancholy who looked as if he were about to cry. "I don't know why things like this keep happening to me," he mumbled as he polished our table with his rag. He handed us menus and turned to leave.

"These are lunch menus. We need breakfast menus," Marita said.

Pierre raised his eyebrows. "Breakfast? We don't serve breakfast after 11:00 a.m. Where do you think you are?" His whole thin frame shook with his question.

We didn't answer.

Tears finally came to Pierre's bespectacled eyes, and as we mentioned eggs Benedict, he began wringing his hands in despair.

"You can't have eggs Benedict, or eggs *anything*."

He turned from us, sagging in depression, and disappeared into the kitchen, never to be seen again. For most people this scene would represent a "very bad day," but when you understand the personalities, this becomes a perfect example.

- The Phlegmatic hostess just didn't care.
- The Choleric boss was too busy to help us.
- The Melancholy waiter left in tears.

As we sat there discussing this fortunate parade of personalities, the manager came back, spotted us sitting there with no food, and said, "Are you still here?"

The answer was obvious. We explained about the waiter's retreat and she said, "I'll go get him and make him come back." This was a vain promise because when she checked up on Pierre she found he had checked out.

"We'll find you another waiter, although I don't know where," she said in a miffed tone.

Off she went into the kitchen, but a minute later she came storming out and headed for the bar. By then we were the only ones left in the whole restaurant. But wait! Here came the manager, towing a fluffy female bartender by the arm.

"Here," she said as she shoved the girl toward us. "There's no one in the bar, so Suzie can be your waitress."

Suzie was Sanguine and didn't care where she was assigned as long as there were people. She had on a low-cut white blouse, tinkling silver strands of beads, and large chandelier earrings that swung as she walked. To top off her look, she wore heavy makeup and had pinned a large red silk rose in her free-styled blonde hair. As we gave her a sweeping survey, she reached over and shook hands with each of us and said brightly, "I'm so happy to see you two. I was so lonely over there with nothing but all those bottles."

She asked us where we were from and was thrilled to find fellow Americans. "I'm from LA myself. My real name is Susannah, but they don't like Southern names up here. So I Frenched it up a bit and changed it to Suzie. I got sick of California, and I came up here to find adventure."

"Did you find any?" I asked. I was soon sorry I asked as she began a long litany of all her disappointing jobs. Finally she took a deep breath and said, "Did you want to eat?"

"When we came in—an hour ago—we thought we wanted breakfast," I said.

"Did you get any?"

"No, the waiter said it was too late."

"It's never too late for breakfast. What do you want?"

"We ordered eggs Benedict, but Pierre said we should have come earlier if we wanted eggs."

"He's really touchy and always goes by the rules. He just can't think outside the box. Believe me, they've got nothing to do in the kitchen. I'll just tell the boys to make two eggs Benedict. They like me in there."

Off Suzie went, with her red rose bouncing in her tousled hair. In no time she was back with two plates of eggs Benedict each decorated with a sprig of parsley on top. She bowed as she set them down. "Ta da! It's magic!"

"When we had finished our meal and left, the Phlegmatic hostess asked if everything was alright," I told our class. "We hesitated and then said, 'Yes, it was just fine.'"

Rose added, "Florence, tell them about our evening at Las Casuelas." She looked at the group. "We didn't know we would be part of a bachelorette party!"

Just the other evening Rose and I went to Las Casuelas, a Mexican restaurant for dinner. At the reservation desk there was the eternal line, but we weren't in a big hurry. As I looked around to see if there were any friends in the Saturday night crowd, I noticed four women all wearing plastic silver crowns sparkling with big, gaudy diamonds. One of the women had a crown with fluffy white tulle sticking out the back.

"We're with royalty!" I pointed out to Rose.

She quickly explained, "That's a new custom. The night before the wedding the girls in the bridal party get all dressed up and go out on the town." I was fascinated with this social tradition I had somehow missed. As Rose and I watched, two of the bridal party went to the ladies' room, and shortly after the host seated the other two in another room. Soon the two emerged from the ladies' room babbling happily away until they realized their friends were gone. "Where are they?" they asked in unison of anyone in the crowd who might know.

I knew. Was it not right for me to take charge? I stepped up and said, "They went into this room here. Come with me."

I led them to their costumed companions, and they all thanked me as if I were the hostess. Soon after, Rose and I were led into the same room and seated back-to-back with my new royal friends. Three bejeweled Sanguines were screaming with joy, and the one Melancholy was sitting quietly, probably wondering why she had this thing on her head and why she was with this rowdy group.

As we finished dinner, I noticed that the bride had persuaded the Phlegmatic busboy to take pictures and—since I was so close and never want to miss a photo op—I couldn't resist turning and posing over the Melancholy's shoulder. The girls didn't see me grinning behind them, so I pointed it out that I was joining the wedding party. We all laughed. Rose and I stood up, formally introduced ourselves, and began giving the girls motherly marriage advice while the busboy busily kept taking pictures.

Someday the husband, whoever he may be, will ask, "Who are these two ladies?" and she—the forgetful Sanguine—will say, "I have no idea."

Our class chuckled as we finished the story.

"After dinner," I continued, "Rose and I began to compare notes about our experiences of the personalities in the food service industry."

"And I remembered a certain family who'd been in the restaurant business," Rose said.

"I was having dinner at the elegant Cork Tree restaurant in Palm Desert, California, with dear friends, Paul and Ronda, both of whom have studied the personalities for years. They'd successfully used this knowledge in understanding their children's temperaments, so I decided to ask if they had any interesting personality stories from their respective workplaces.

"Ronda, a licensed marriage and family therapist, told me she had 'a million of them' but had to keep them confidential. Too bad. They might have boosted sales of our book! So I then asked Paul, 'You used to work in a restaurant. In your opinion, who makes the best waiter or waitress?'"

He thought for a minute.

"That's easy. Someone who can tell about the personalities of the diners. The Cholerics need your immediate attention, the Sanguines need to see you smile, and the Melancholies need you to be humble if you forget or make a mistake. The Phlegmatics will forgive you if you make a mistake because they see how hard you are working, and they sure don't want to be doing your job!"

Ronda added that that was what had made their daughter Rachel the top server at the local upscale steak house. "Rachel was raised on the personalities. From body language, speech, and attitudes she can usually figure out her customers' personalities right away, and she makes sure to keep track of what they need."

Paul gave some good, bottom-line advice when he said, "The customer is there for a pleasant experience, not just food. If you can't see what their emotional as well as their dietary needs are, then in a certain sense you've left them on their own. That's what makes good servers: not just taking care of food orders but taking care of people."

"Good. But how about a specific story?"

Paul smiled. "Okay. Here's a good one."

Choleric Paul was only eighteen when he was made manager at a now-defunct but popular chain restaurant the Red Baron. The airplane-themed eateries were located in airports and were frequented by pilots, other airline employees, travelers, and guests. Because of Paul's Midwest work ethic and strong Choleric drive, he found himself in charge of and supervising much older men and women.

"It was hard to get their respect," Paul recalls. "Some of them could have been my parents, and I'm sure they thought, *Why should we listen to* this *young punk?* But one day that all changed."

Paul told how he'd often walk back into the kitchen to find cooks, busboys, and even waitresses having huge food fights. Big mess, extra cost, and wasted time! Still a teenager, Paul reprimanded the lot and warned that if they did not stop he would fire them all on the spot. Some seemed to listen, but there were more than a few loud guffaws and muffled snickers that Paul chose to ignore.

"Sunday brunch was our biggest moneymaker. One Sunday morning I came through the back door into the kitchen and yes . . . another food fight! So I knew I had to back up my promise to fire them all on the spot. But then I thought, *Uh-oh, if I fire everyone who will cook the food and do the dishes? The place is packed!* But Cholerics never let that stop them. So I fired them all. Cooks. Dishwashers. Waitresses. Just like I'd said.

"At first they didn't believe it. But I called in the bookkeeper to issue pink slips, and within minutes they were all gone. So there I was, all alone with a full dining room to feed. I put on an apron, started cooking, and ran the rest of the kitchen . . . BY MYSELF . . . the rest of the day. I was exhausted, but no one ever questioned my authority again!"

Everyone in the room laughed when Rose finished her story, and then Howard spoke out.

"Hey, Rose. You're not going to believe this, but I know Paul. We went to a food service convention once and sat together for the whole weekend. I remember him telling me that story. He lives out in the desert, right?"

"Wow, Howard, what a small world. Yes, he does!"

"Did he tell you about the time the SWAT team was called in to his restaurant? Now *that's* a story!"

"Howard! I was just about to tell that story. But since you are Sanguine, and we have been learning about what good storytellers they can be, why don't *you* tell it?"

Howard beamed and started right in.

"Well, when Paul was manager at the Red Baron, one of his waitresses was a cute little sixteen-year-old who was acting as the hostess one day. A man came in, grabbed the girl, pulled out a gun, and screamed, 'Everyone get down! I need a pilot. Is anyone in here a pilot?' He was looking for a quick way out of the country. Paul, being Choleric, quickly lunged forward to save the girl, and not thinking it through first, found himself staring down the barrel of a .38-caliber Smith and Wesson. He backed off, and then the man ran out the door dragging the girl. I bet the hostess was Phlegmatic, because I remember Paul said she was very compliant." He paused for a minute and added, "But I guess everyone gets compliant when they're facing the possibility of death! Right?"

Howard took a big breath and then stood up and walked around the room to finish his dramatic story. "Paul called 911 and then ran down the back stairwell to see if he could do something for his hostess! He told me the guy had a crazy look in his eyes and he was nervous and sweaty. The cops arrived quickly, and their police cars were all around the airport runways. The man had hijacked a car to drive out to an airliner, and he'd taken the girl hostage with him into the plane.

"But then the SWAT team did what they do best. They saw the man sitting in the cockpit, away from the girl, and they fired a long-distance shot right through the window and straight through his temple. BOOM! Dead. Blood and brains all over the window. Paul saw it all."

When Howard finished the group was silent. Howard was now standing next to me in the front of the room, satisfactorily survey-ing the reactions of his rapt audience. I thanked him for a story well told and asked, "Okay, Sanguine Howard. Any part of that tale *not* true?"

Howard sighed and smiled. "Okay. You got me, Florence. Paul never told me what type of gun it was, so I filled that part in."

I laughed and led Howard back to his chair. "Filled that part in! Okay you Melancholies. Make sure to get the Sanguines the details or they will *fill that part in*! And you don't want to have that in *your* workplace!"

Dr. Hastings made a little noise in his throat. "Yes, no Sanguines in the operating room!"

Rose agreed. "And that's exactly what we'll cover in our next class, Dr. Hastings. Personalities in the medical field. And I won't bore you today with the story of how my doctor brother, Fred, invited me to observe one of his surgeries and I was a little upset that I had to take off my gold hoop earrings before I suited up!"

Holly howled.

What Did We Learn This Time?

If you're the server:

- If the Sanguines want something special, smile and give it to them!
- If service is delayed, apologize and give the Cholerics a discount.
- If the Melancholies aren't pleased, agree and take it back to the kitchen.
- If the Phlegmatics can't make up their mind, make some recommendations.

If you're the diner:

- Tell the Sanguine they're cute. You'll get a free dessert!

- Thank the Choleric for working so hard to take care of you.
- Be patient with the Melancholy. It's the kitchen that didn't get it right!
- Be specific with the Phlegmatic, and don't get irritated if you have to ask twice.

14

Personalities in Health Services

At our next session, I (Florence) hadn't even started class when Dr. Hastings raised his hand and began speaking. The other students hurried to sit down.

"Florence, I know today we're talking about personalities in health services. Since this is a field in which I've been active most of my life, I'd like to share *my* observations about what personalities work well in the medical field." He paused, looked at Howard, and added with a kind smile, "And that might even include Sanguines." Melancholy humor can be dry but refreshing.

"I've brought a summary of my thoughts that I think might be helpful. And I made copies for everyone. May I read it?"

Since our first class, Dr. Hastings and I had developed a comfortable relationship. I knew he was intelligent and I was sure his list of observations was perfect. I also knew that he would not try to take over the whole class, so I agreed to use his material to begin the day's teaching.

"Yes, I think we'd all like to hear what you've come up with. Let's all take a look at what Dr. Hastings has brought us today," Rose said and started helping to pass the papers around.

"I didn't make it in color, like I know you might have, Florence," he said. "But I think you'll all find it without error."

"Without error! Of course!" said Howard with a big smile. "We sure do need brilliant doctors. You know, that makes me realize something: people come to my table to eat and have a good time, but when they get up on *your* table, well, the fun and games need to be over."

Good-natured Howard gave Dr. Hastings a deeply appreciative glance, and the rest of the group nodded.

Dr. Hastings' Observations

The best doctor/dentist is . . . Melancholy. They paid better attention in medical school and often remember more detail than the other personalities. They need to access that information—sometimes in a hurry—when a patient needs urgent care.

- They work more slowly and carefully than the other personalities.
- They suspect and detect hidden problems that others may have overlooked.
- They seek perfection in what they do.

The best nurse/assistant is . . . Phlegmatic. They are kind, caring, gentle, understanding, and cooperative. They don't try to make light of pain or problems, and they are excellent at listening. They are extremely patient with patients, especially with the elderly. They work hard and do exactly what they are told.

- They don't get ruffled when the doctor yells at them (or at least they are smart enough to hide it).

196

- They take their time with patients, never rushing them through.
- Even their physical demeanor is nonthreatening and safe.

The best office manager is . . . Choleric. The rest of the nursing or support staff can be caring, gentle, and detail-oriented, but they can also move so slowly that everything gets behind. Patients will be waiting too long and everyone will be cranky. The Choleric will step in and keep things moving at a good pace.

- They see the big picture of how things should go in the office each day.
- They are ready to problem solve at a minute's notice.
- They don't get too worried about getting their feelings hurt; they'd rather get the job done.

The best office receptionist is . . . Sanguine. Whether the Sanguine is a male or female, that sunny smile somehow helps the patient feel a bit better when their insurance won't cover the procedure! The Sanguines help to soften the clinical, antiseptic feeling that—by necessity—some offices or hospitals have.

- They make good aides if they don't have to have too much technical responsibility.
- They are encouraging and uplifting to worried family members and are good with children.
- They make light of the uptight Melancholy doctor and help everyone in the office have a good—and sometimes necessary—laugh.

"Excellent observations," I said. "Thank you, Doctor. Today we're going to be sharing a few other medical stories we received from our Personality Trainers around the country. See if you can relate to any of them, and then before we leave today we'll hand out a helpful chart."

Nikki's "Specimens"

Nikki was one of those who called us to share her story. Sometimes she thinks the different personalities are like little people in a petri dish.

"I live near Atlanta, the home of the Centers for Disease Control, where medical professionals study how patients respond to the presence of germs. I realize that every hospital is like a big laboratory where you can observe how patients respond to the other personalities as if *they* were the bacteria!"

Nikki makes a good point. Too often we look at the opposite personalities as if they were pestilent pests, boring bacteria, or virulent viruses out to attack us and make our lives miserable. But understanding the natural strengths and emotional needs of others can help cure our bad attitude.

Nikki went on to say, "Recently my mom had a health scare that brought us all to the hospital. We were like living personality specimens, floating around in the cardiology unit with a host of hospital staff." Her descriptions below of the "specimens" are insightful.

Specimen # 1: My Mom, the Sanguine Patient

Mom was admitted with extreme lethargy and shortness of breath, which could not dampen her spirits because she was the center of attention and had a captive audience! As always, she made the best out of an otherwise scary situation with her optimistic, appealing, and talkative personality. I could see her physically and emotionally responding to everyone who entered her room as if each person were some form of medication.

Her Phlegmatic cardiologist offered her calm, quiet sympathy and assurance, but Mom responded better to her "visits" from Michelle, the cute, bubbly Sanguine nurse who expressed enthusiasm and interest in Mom's endless stories.

198

The Melancholy nurses entered as caregivers doing their duty rather than as friends who would forge lifelong relationships. They had no fuzzy animals hanging from their stethoscopes, but they did make sure that my mom's vital signs were updated on the whiteboard—something the Sanguines always seemed to neglect in their excitement over her teddy bear's latest fashion statement.

But Mom's upbeat mood would be immediately dashed when the Choleric physician's assistant would stride into her room, clipboard in hand, demanding quick answers to medical questions. He was not interested in her stories or her bear. He wanted "just the facts, ma'am," before he bulldozed on to the next patient.

Specimen #2: My Father, the Choleric

From Mom's first symptom, Dad wanted to take charge, especially being the loving spouse of the patient. But overwhelmed by other personalities, Dad was pushed aside while Mom was poked and prodded. He could only sit and listen to the staff telling him to wait for the next test results. The more powerless he felt, the more impatient and frustrated he became. Dealing all morning with the distracted energy of the Sanguine nurse added to his irritation, but Dad responded well to his fellow Choleric, the clipboard-carrying PA, and Dr. Phlegmatic actually helped calm Dad down, since he gave strong, steady, and intelligent assurance that all was well and under control. The Melancholy nurse in charge kept him well informed with the details of my mom's care, which he greatly appreciated.

Specimen #3: My Brother, the Phlegmatic

My brother was happily reconciled to being hundreds of miles away from the whole situation, participating through daily phone calls. Because he is a good listener, we could vent our frustrations to him and then laugh at his responses that were full of dry humor and insight. Although he stayed at home, I think he would have been just as happy to be with us, since Mom's room had a remote control, cable television, and a recliner that unfolded into a bed.

Specimen #4: Melancholy Me

I am the "perfect" Melancholy daughter and the member of the family who has studied Florence's *Personality Plus* materials. I love research and was fascinated by the microcosm of personalities flowing through this small hospital room.

I noticed and admired immediately the perfect, detailed charting of my fellow Melancholies but was drained by the never-ending energy of the Sanguines. The insensitivity of the Cholerics hurt my feelings, and the laid-back delays of the Phlegmatics frustrated my desire for timeliness. But instead of crawling into my shell, as I might normally do, I decided to put my knowledge of the personalities to work:

I entertained my Sanguine mom by creating teddy bear fashions out of surgical supplies, turning them into conversation centerpieces.

I completely supported my dad's daily decisions, such as restaurant choices and driving routes, allowing him to feel in charge.

I did not push my Phlegmatic brother to make the trip to be with us, knowing that he had enough on his plate at home.

And I was content to keep order in the room by watering flowers and picking up alcohol swabs and syringe covers off the floor (probably dropped by Sanguine nurses!).

"So what did I learn?" Nikki concluded. "That just a few dollars invested in learning personalities is worth thousands spent on pharmaceuticals. You don't need a pill to help others feel better when you know their personality. And the benefits to everyone are endless. Thank you so much for showing us how to sort out the individuals in family or friends and do a personality profile on each one. Instead of branding them as peculiar we can accept them as they are and find them much more lovable than they used to be."

Melancholies in the Medical Field

Another letter we received was from Annie, a Phlegmatic-Melancholy combination who was head nurse in a local hospital for twenty-five years. She was adept at keeping everyone calm (Phlegmatic) during emergencies and made sure that things were according to hospital procedure (Melancholy). When she retired, she worked part-time in a cosmetic surgeon's office. He was "mega-Melancholy," and Annie shared what was good and bad about working for him.

Just a few dollars invested in learning personalities is worth thousands spent on pharmaceuticals. You don't need a pill to help others feel better when you know their personality.

"Let's say a patient was coming in for a face-lift. We'd schedule the typical amount of time for that—say two hours—and make sure the necessary nursing and after-care staff was also scheduled. But once the patient was on the table, and the doctor saw that he needed to go slower or work longer on a certain area to get it just right, he'd sometimes go two hours over the allotted time. The patient looked perfect afterward, but we were exhausted. None of the nurses ever really knew how long they would be at work. That put a lot of stress on our families as well. And—the worst part—he refused to pay us overtime!"

Annie shared that his Melancholy desire for perfection made him one of the most sought-after plastic surgeons in the state, but to this day he still has a hard time keeping his staff. But she also admitted, "I guess that's not because he's Melancholy . . . it's that he's cheap!"

Rose shared a story about her brother, who is a respected surgeon in the Midwest.

"My brother Fred is a perfect Melancholy with a secondary Phlegmatic personality. I saw the particular strength of the Melancholy in action when I was observing a minor surgery with him once. A young boy had sliced open his leg just below the knee in a playground accident a few days before. He'd been stitched up in the ER and sent home. But a few days later he had a high fever and his wound was inflamed. When my brother reopened the stitches, he saw that the wound had not been completely cleaned out . . . there was still gravel in the boy's leg.

"So—in a teaching moment—Fred turned and asked the assistant medical students what they thought the best way to fix the problem was. One suggested cutting more deeply into the leg, opening the flaps of skin wide like a book and really getting in and thoroughly cleaning out the wound. Fred replied that sounded good at first, but if they thought about it, it would make a bigger scar and introduce the possibility of more infection as the wound healed. He explained that solutions in healing the human body are like mysteries to be solved. They deserve deep thinking, even 'outside the box.'

"I listened in awe as Fred explained that they should cut a very tiny hole down at the end of the area where the gravel was still under the skin and insert what I thought looked like a Waterpik. Instead of making a larger cut, Fred instructed a medical student to take over and flush the debris gently with water out the small hole. It would have the same effect but save tissue and lessen the scarring. Fred supervised as the student finished and then stitched up the patient. It was amazing!"

Rose shared that it is often the Melancholy practitioner or researcher who dares to think of ways to solve problems that no one else can see or even imagine at first; the Choleric surgeon might rush to take the fastest route, the Phlegmatic might choose the easiest way. Where is the Sanguine? They didn't finish medical school, but they are over at the nurse's station ordering flowers and get-well balloons for your room!

"Fred is the youngest in our large family," Rose added. "He grew up with all of the different personalities. He learned to get along with bossy Choleric brothers and sisters and a flighty Sanguine—me. He understands the other siblings who are Melancholies and Phlegmatics. I also think that's why he's such a good doctor: he understands his patients and knows how to communicate with each personality."

We want to help you better understand your patients, too. If you're working in the medical, dental, or other health services field, you have the opportunity to improve relationships with co-workers by employing the tips and techniques we've shared so far. And you can also get along better with the patients who come to you for help.

Loving Them All

Our last word for you in the medical field is the story of Patch Adams, a folk hero and a pacifist with a fake red nose, whose life was the basis of the film *Patch Adams* (1998) starring Robin Williams. He's also a medical doctor who's a gentle Phlegmatic and a caring Melancholy. Each year he organizes a group of volunteers from around the world to travel to various countries where they dress in costume to entertain and bring hope to orphans, patients, and others who need love and attention. More importantly, Dr. Adams claims to be an expert in the art of love and care.

Speaking at a convention of professional caregivers in Palm Springs, California, Dr. Adams gave smart advice on how to avoid burnout in *any* business. "If you don't want to burn out, fall in love," Adams told the crowd. "Fall in love with your family and your patients."

Fall in love? That's hard to do when we're trapped in an over-worked and stressed-out culture, where anyone in any business can develop an attitude that the customer, client, or co-worker is a burden, not a blessing. But resenting others for their differences and wishing and hoping they'd change will only keep us from reaching our goals. True business success comes when we not only appreciate people's different temperaments but also begin to truly see them as a blessing in our life—we "fall in love" with them. So after learning about the natural gifts each temperament brings to the world, what is the best business advice of all?

Perhaps it is this: when it comes to personalities, *we should love them all.*

What Did We Learn This Time?

On pages 205–6 there's a helpful chart for working with patients.

As we showed the group this helpful chart and stayed late to answer their questions, we realized how our pupils had grown up. We genuinely cared for each other and we sincerely wanted to learn more each week. They were applying their new information to their respective careers and were already seeing results.

After the class left, Rose and I gave each other a big hug and said almost together, "It's better than we ever thought it could be and we've fallen in love with them all."

Working with Patients in Health Services

Popular Sanguine	Powerful Choleric
A popular Sanguine's basic desire is fun. Being seriously ill says, "Life is no fun." Try to give them some type of fun.	A powerful Choleric's basic desire is control. Being incapacitated says, "Life is out of my control." Allow them to make decisions.

Sanguines need:
- positive and cheerful personnel
- pleasant surroundings and environment: pictures, flowers, music, satin pillowcases
- good listeners, for they need to talk
- physical touch and loving support, to feel that you really enjoy caring for them
- people, because they dislike being alone; parties perk them up
- compliments and encouragement
- instructions given more than once (they tend to forget)
- directions on priorities—which pills are essential
- attractive appearance—help with hair or wig, nails, makeup, and a pretty gown or attractive robe

Cholerics need:
- to be allowed to be independent as much as possible because they want to do for themselves
- facts as soon as possible for quick decision making, no cover-up
- intelligent medical personnel (they are bored by repetition and by incompetence)
- freedom of movement if possible; it is most difficult for them to be confined
- choice in selection of treatments
- room where they can see the activity in the hall or out of a window
- prompt attention to problems
- procedures done expediently; don't dally
- sense of loyalty from medical staff
- praise for how well they are doing

Peaceful Phlegmatic	Perfect Melancholy
A peaceful Phlegmatic's basic desire is to avoid conflict and confrontation. They will deny serious illness; it overwhelms them. Being sick says, "You've got to face this serious problem and make hard choices."	A perfect Melancholy's basic desire is to have everything done correctly. Being ill says, "Nothing's ever going to be right again." Don't try to jolly them up but allow them to grieve.

Phlegmatics need:
- a peaceful room and surroundings
- time for themselves to think it through
- encouragement to express feelings and fears
- TV, books, and environment where they can "people watch"
- motivation to make decisions and to move into action
- extra time for eating, doing personal care, and decision making
- nonthreatening and congenial personnel
- not to be neglected in their care due to their congenial ways
- feelings of respect and self-worth

Melancholies need:
- things done right the first time; don't deviate from the tried-and-true method
- a schedule for their plan of care, lab tests, X-rays, treatments, and baths
- things organized and prepared when having blood drawn, IVs started, and treatments
- medication on time and schedule followed
- telephone, call light, personal items convenient and where they want them
- adequate time allowed in eating, bathing, and filling out menus
- ample time to study drug sheets, new information, consent forms before making decisions
- call lights answered promptly
- correct and factual information given to answer their questions
- a good listener and attention to their complaints
- feeling of sensitive and competent support

15

Personalities in Retail/Office

I (Rose) was writing on the whiteboard when the students came in and took their places. Florence started out by pointing to what I had written, saying, "Good morning. Rose has a reminder on the board, something I'm sure you all know by now. I suggest you write it down." Everyone looked up to read:

Personalities and Profits Are Directly Related

Florence continued. "When profits are down, you may not have a business problem—you probably have a personality problem." Then she looked at Pastor Paul and schoolteacher Carmen. "Some of you may be less worried about financial profits than educational or spiritual profits. But they are all the same. Whether you're buying or selling, preaching or healing, it's understanding people that will make your endeavors successful or not."

I nodded. "Florence and I have many examples from those whom we've interviewed about how they used knowledge of the personalities to succeed at work."

"Our first example covers many areas and touches on problems familiar to those who work with an absent or too-busy manager. When a Choleric friend of mine stepped into a near impossible situation of untrained and unsupervised staff, I asked her to put it all down on paper," Florence said. "Because she is a Choleric who loves challenges and a Melancholy who sees the failures quickly, she was the one for the job."

Florence and I handed out copies of her story:

I was both excited and anxious on my first day as manager of a national company that provided a mail-order product. There were ten employees, eight of whom were only part-time, working odd and assorted shifts—assuming they came to work at all. I'd been hired—and given the authority—to assess operations and make necessary changes. I came in, sat down, looked around me, and thought, *What have I gotten myself into?*

The entire workplace was crowded with piles of boxes, desks overflowed with papers, and there was clutter on every available surface. I was astounded! I took a deep breath and decided to wait and observe before I took any action.

Before I assessed the people, I had to do something about this mess! On the first Saturday I arrived in my work clothes and began cleaning and throwing out old brochures, boxes, and stacks of useless items. I even scrubbed the bathroom from top to bottom. When the staff arrived Monday morning, I announced that things would stay this way from now on. A clean and tidy environment would benefit us all.

Then I turned my attention to the staff. I'm sure they were afraid I would "clean house" there, too, and fire them all, but my only goal was to discover their natural strengths and weaknesses to support the needs of the organization.

I started with the mail room, where orders were shipped once each afternoon. A young Phlegmatic high school student had been put in charge and arrived each day at noon to prepare the day's shipments. Many days I would see him leaning back in his chair, feet propped up on the worktable, staring out into space. His life was full of daily activities that included his friends, school, music, athletics, and youth group. I was not surprised when I learned that often he came in late or had some excuse for not showing up at all. That left a big burden on someone else who wasn't trained in mail room procedures to get product out to customers.

I had a little chat with him, telling him how important his position was and how everyone depended on his ability to get the products mailed each day. I insisted he arrive every day and on time. Soon after that he told us he just could not keep up his school activities and work too. He resigned.

Our other Phlegmatic part-timer was a young man hired to take inventory and be available for miscellaneous tasks. He, too, liked leaning back in his chair, and when he was bored he'd ride his chair up and down the hallways. It's not that there was no work to do, but he thought it was just "too physical" and required too much effort. One day the entire staff was working to move, load, and unload heavy boxes of inventory. Someone's mother had even showed up that day and was helping out. We noticed that this fellow was resting in his chair, and I asked him how he could just sit there and let an elderly woman work.

"I'm tired," he said. With increased pressure on him to actually work, he soon left to find another job that would allow him to relax in the daytime and play in a band at night.

I'd hoped these two would have worked harder, but now they were gone. Who else would make it, and who would leave? The product manager was the next to go.

He'd started with the company as a service clerk and was attending a local college with a business major. He had no experience for his position but had been thrust into management when the former manager left to get married. He was given a manager compensation package and put in charge of all inventory and shipping. I learned that there were large financial losses in this area, and in one of our first meetings I asked him for a cost analysis of the shipping expenses. He stared at me with a blank look on his face. He had no idea what I was talking about. When I advised him that there were big problems that needed to be fixed, he simply replied, "Oh well, mistakes happen."

Since I understood the personalities and knew that arguing would not work with him, we issued a new policy that deducted the cost of shipping errors from commission payments. That's all it took. He left to go work at a retail store, and I found out later he also changed his college major from business to philosophy.

It's not just Phlegmatics, though, who can struggle to fit into the workplace. One Choleric staff member was also part-time, working on weekends since this was her second job. If things didn't go her way, she became insolent and refused to cooperate with others. She could be bossy and abrasive and often told the clients what *they* needed to do to help *her*. She had no office authority, but she actually "fired" someone in the office who would not do things her way. As a result, the other staff personnel spent a lot of time mending fences and smoothing ruffled feathers. Once I began to establish some guidelines for her on customer relations, she began to look for other work where no one would challenge her. She didn't last long.

A Sanguine in our front office was a delightful customer service assistant, but he didn't know how to use the computer and did not want to learn. That was just no fun! He'd also pick and choose the days he showed up for work. If the other fun people on the staff were not there that day, he'd tell us he just couldn't come in.

Our bookkeeper was also a lovely Sanguine woman, but she told me right off that she knew nothing about bookkeeping and had simply been hired one day when she came in to have lunch with her friend who worked there. Everyone knew they would have to remind her when payday was coming so she could remember to do payroll. Imagine—a bookkeeper who couldn't keep books!

The new company policies were taking all of the fun out of work for these employees. As it became clearer over time that the party was over, many of the part-time employees began to drift off into the sunset—but they didn't all leave. The changes that called for increased accountability began to produce fruit. When the product sales manager left, we hired a strong Choleric woman to take her place. She went immediately to work developing systems to eliminate shipping errors. She created a more efficient inventory system, kept an eagle eye on costs, and turned the losses into large profits. The more she accomplished, the harder she worked—a true Choleric trait. Everyone was happy, especially me. I didn't have to babysit all these loose, free-thinking children anymore.

Another employee, a college student who was a Phlegmatic-Sanguine, also began to blossom. He was bright, friendly, and a good worker. But as is common with Phlegmatics, he waited to be told what to do. Since I understood his need to feel valuable and important, I decided to engage him rather than push him. I was sitting in the front office—making myself visible rather than staying behind closed doors—and working on some product costs. I invited him to join me.

"Take out your calculator," I said. He did as I asked. I gave him some numbers, and he reported the total. It was a negative. We were losing money on the item in question. I knew the solution, but I asked for his advice.

He laughed and suggested we should just give the product away, but then he took the challenge, thought about it, and replied, "We need to increase the price to cover costs."

It was a good start, but we knew we could not do this and continued together to solve the problem. By working together we found a way to lower costs. I could have done this on my own in less time, but now this young man had learned something valuable and had pride of ownership in this business decision.

Perhaps the greatest blessing was when a previous bookkeeper returned. She was Choleric-Sanguine. Sanguines don't necessarily like complex math, but a Choleric loves to take over a mess and put things in order. Having control over the money gave her a feeling of power. She kept us on target with the finances. When we could not afford something, she told us. If we were over budget, she told us. If we made a bad business decision, she told us. This type of bottom-line, up-front communication can be hard to hear for some, but because she was also a Sanguine, she gave it a light touch too. As a manager who wanted to do a good job, I deeply appreciated her candor, her insistence that we all do things right, and her upbeat attitude each morning.

In a matter of three months we went from ten employees who came and went when they felt like it to two full-time employees and one part-time worker. I hadn't fired a single one; I'd just insisted on some accountability. We tightened up production, reduced costs, and created a dynamic team that worked together toward common goals. And this was all because of an understanding of the strengths, weaknesses, and emotional needs of the personalities, and the strength to put this knowledge into action.

Winning at Wal-Mart

"Another friend called me," Florence said, "and asked how she could do a better job in training her employees. Cindy managed a Wal-Mart optometry department with typical retail problems. After she and I went over her situation, and she made changes, I asked her to tell me what she did. She had a series of staff meetings and taught the personalities to the staff so they could understand themselves, their co-workers, and their customers."

Cindy started with Abby, the perfect one. This Melancholy is excellent at details, notices if a pair of eyeglasses is missing from the rack, and gets all her duties done on time and perfectly. She puts on her white coat as required each morning and gives the impression that she could do surgery on you if required. Cindy came up with an idea to keep children amused while their parents were getting their eyes examined. Abby took the idea and built a contest around it with prizes that she administers. She gives the children a list of different items and sends them into the store to find the price of each one. When they return with their list filled out, they get a prize. Not only does this keep the children from being pests, but they become prizewinners as well. Also, when Mother needs new glasses, the child is eager to return to Wal-Mart.

Dee is a Choleric and is working toward becoming board certified. She arrives on time and can do every job in the department better than anyone else. She does her work quickly and motivates the others to action. You might hear her say, "While we have a quiet moment, let's polish the countertops." She hands each employee a cloth and they get to work. If anyone gets lazy, Dee has only to say, "Cindy will be back in a minute," and they all snap to it. She functions in her Choleric strength and has learned to curb her impatience.

Creative Sanguine Cheri loves her job. It's party time for her every day, even though she never knows who is coming to the workday festivities. She doesn't like to wear the white coat because it covers up her forever-new party dress. She welcomes all customers as though they are her best friends and hugs them when they leave. "Come on back. I'll be looking for you," she says. Of course, as a Sanguine, she can't remember them very long, but they think she will.

Melancholy customers don't like Cheri. She's too bubbly and cheerful. As one said, "She can't be for real." And sometimes she isn't. If she doesn't know the answer, she makes one up. She "quotes" store policy when there isn't one. If customers return, they will often refer to what Cheri told them the last time. Because the staff loves her, they don't say, "That's ridiculous!" Instead they reply, "Well, that's close," and then they move on to the truth. Since they're all willing to cover for her shortcomings, they wonder, *What will happen to Cheri if she ever gets a real job?*

When Cindy has a day off or is going on vacation, she makes a large chart for Cheri with daily instructions. Cheri checks them off and adds notes: "Came in ten minutes early!" or "Replaced paper cups just before they ran out!" When Cindy returns, Cheri—as a child would show her mother—directs her to the chart full of arrows, notes, and happy faces. She is so proud of what she has accomplished.

213

Cindy said, "I have learned to get excited over her report and praise her for her grand achievements. When I told her I filed her completed charts for posterity, she began to draw fewer cartoons and wrote more lavish praises of herself." Cindy compliments her, even for emptying a wastebasket. The others don't mind. They just shrug their shoulders and say, "Cheri needs it." Because Cindy has shared with them all what she knows about personalities, they understand Cheri and enjoy her humor and her new clothes.

A new employee was recently sent to Cindy by the Human Resources Department. She is Destiny, a teenager who is still in training. Cindy says, "Training for who knows what!" She is Phlegmatic, laid back, and unused to rules or discipline. She doesn't understand terms like "company procedures" or "work ethic," and each day Cindy has to re-explain what Destiny's job really is. Cindy appreciates Destiny's calm presence and lack of intense emotions or high drama, but her immaturity keeps Destiny from blossoming into a balanced Phlegmatic. She tends to hide behind the showcase and text-message her boyfriend, who is currently unemployed. Her ultimate goal in life is to get married, hope he gets a job, and live happily ever after. Cindy hopes that happens soon.

Last on the list is Jim, a twenty-year-old college student. When he is on duty, there is an air of excitement among the staff. The customers think he's adorable, and his only problem is they think he's too young to really know anything. However, once he has handled their problem with charm and efficiency, they love him and want only Jim to wait on them next time. Cindy's uncle—who used to want only her to take care of his needs—now asks for Jim. "He's the best," he says. Jim is Choleric (*let's get this job done now!*) and Sanguine (*but let's have fun doing it*).

Cindy feels like a ringmaster in a circus. "If I didn't understand the personalities, who knows how I'd master this group? This is a great company, but now I know why so many managers just quit."

214

"Wal-Mart should have Cindy train all their managers, and perhaps fewer would suddenly leave," Florence quipped, as she finished the story.

Winning at Wig-Wam

"A friend of mine owns the Wig-Wam, a retail store with hundreds of Styrofoam heads and wigs along the wall shelves—blonde, brunette, redhead, short, long, and even punk styles," I began. "The ladies who work there often say, 'We have a head for everybody!' . . . and they do."

When Florence and I asked if they would give us stories about personalities in their workplace, they all pointed to the heads on the walls. "We call them 'the girls.' They are the ones with personality! Each one has a personality according to her hairstyle. We think they wait until we lock up at night to have an all-night party. Sometimes when we come into the shop in the morning, the heads are in different places. It's like they went visiting with each other and when the daylight came, they just stayed there." Clearly these ladies enjoy working in their shop.

Georgia is the managing salesperson and a bright Choleric who enjoys helping women shop for just the right hairstyle. "Most women come in wanting to look like some movie star and will point to a wig on the wall. 'I want to look like her.' But I know I'll never be able to make them look that good. I try my best, but they'll try to tell me something must be wrong with the wig. Once I finally got tired of being polite with a very rude and pushy customer. I blurted out, 'Ma'am, we can change your hair but we can't change your face!'"

Everyone howled. Another saleswoman who joined in our conversation added, "Yeah, I've told some of the really nasty customers, 'This is a comb, not a magic wand!'" More laughter.

215

But then Georgia got serious and told the story of an angry Choleric man who came into the break room and yelled at her. "He'd walked in with his timid wife and looked around. The other ladies were busy with customers, and he was extremely impatient. He stormed back into the break room where I was having lunch. I looked up—still chewing my sandwich—and saw him point his finger at me."

"YOU!" he yelled. "Get up and get out here. NOW! My wife needs a wig! You're being very rude just sitting back here wasting time."

Georgia quickly recovered her initial shock and held up her hand—policeman style—shooting the same Choleric energy right back at him. In a firm voice she told him, "Sir, *you* have to leave. NOW!"

The man was startled and then quickly changed his tone. "I'm sorry. I'm so sorry. My wife and I just came from the doctor's office where we found out she has cancer. I think I'm still in shock. I guess I'm having a hard time dealing with the emotions." He suddenly became quiet.

Georgia realized that there was a person behind this angry personality. She got up, smiled gently, and walked with him back to the shop floor and welcomed his wife into her chair. "Don't worry," she told the man. "You can have a seat, and I'll make sure I take good care of your wife."

"Georgia's story illustrates both the strengths and weaknesses of the Choleric temperament. In any workplace, the Choleric intensity to barge in and boss others around is a weakness and often fueled by an interior emotional struggle. Georgia's ability to quickly set a firm boundary with him was a natural Choleric strength. We learned that day that there is often a hidden problem under Choleric anger and that Styrofoam heads have personalities!"

"Florence? If you don't mind, I'd like to close our class with the story from Chico's," I said.

I stepped forward and began. Chico's is one of the women's boutique chains where Florence and I love to shop together. I told the class, "If you're in retail, take a clue from a Sanguine shopper!"

I had barely finished my sentence when Fran Taylor laughed and blurted out, "I think I know exactly where you're going with this one! Sanguines are suckers for a sale, right?"

"Right," I said. "It's not to save money but to get two shirts for the price of one! But value-minded Melancholies are also suckers for a sale. What I'd like to share is how I think that a Phlegmatic might just make the best salesperson, even though I didn't used to think that. If you're like me, you've run into lazy Phlegmatic clerks who just didn't care, or depressed Melancholies who only wanted to go home."

We saw several heads nod.

I reminded them that when any of the personalities are unhappy they will always work in their weaknesses. "I'll never forget one day Florence and I went to Chico's," I said. "A content, balanced Phlegmatic woman waited on us. I don't think she ever read *Personality Plus*, but she sure understood personalities and because of that she rang up one of the biggest sales of the year. She wasn't a sparkling Sanguine or a fast-talking Choleric. She was cool, calm, and smart. She read me like a book."

Florence was over in the sale section, and I was trying on gold cuff bracelets. I was in a bad mood because I hadn't been making any money lately, and that made my Choleric side angry and frustrated. I'd already told Florence I would accompany her to the store but I wasn't buying anything today. The practical voice in my head said, *Why are you here even* thinking *about spending more money? You should just go over and tell Florence how cute she looks and stop looking around.* But the Sanguine side of me was feeling sorry and saying, *Those gold earrings would look gorgeous with that bracelet. You want it. You deserve it!*

A Choleric saleswoman walked right up to me and practically yelled, "Everything is half off. And today it's buy one, get one free. You need to get that bracelet. . . . It looks great on you!" But her quick, rehearsed sales pitch irritated me. I gave her a curt Choleric smile and walked away.

A few minutes later the same peaceful, Phlegmatic saleswoman I'd seen at first approached me slowly and stood next to me.

"You have beautiful hair," the saleswoman said sweetly. "Do you do it yourself?"

Uh-oh. I felt myself soften. I grinned, and the class chuckled. "She wasn't trying to sell me anything (or was she?). She knew exactly what to say to the Sanguine who wants everyone to think she's pretty, and to say so!

"Thank you. Well, I do cut my own bangs, but my stylist does a good job." She was so sweet and inoffensive and I wondered what other nice thing she might say to me. Would she be my new friend?

"Well, you're a beautiful woman. I'm Nancy. I see you're wearing a Chico's outfit today. You should be a model for Chico's!"

"Not me!" I protested. *She thinks I'm pretty. I like her. I'm feeling better now. Maybe I can afford just a little something.*

"If I'm bothering you, please let me know. It's just that if you like those cropped pants you're wearing, we have some over here that would look adorable on you." I followed Nancy like a lamb being led to the slaughter.

Then Nancy did something even smarter. She quietly rallied a few of the other salesladies who were just standing around to come over and admire me. (Phlegmatics don't try to do it all themselves like Cholerics. They know the power of a combined effort.) That was it. I was finished.

After Nancy—and the other ladies—suggested more pants, matching tops, and cute jackets, I followed them back to the jewelry section for accessories. At the cash register—where the grand total had reached great proportions—I decided to look around for

Florence. She was on the other side of the store, and I noticed she, too, was surrounded by several saleswomen who were oohing and ahhing over whatever she was holding up in the mirror. The lovely lions had moved in for the kill.

"Even though Florence and I have a practical Choleric side, when it comes to shopping we do not want to be told what to buy. We are not that interested in fabric content; we can figure that out for ourselves. We don't want to hear your sales pitch. If it makes us look good, who cares about saving money? Where a Melancholy might shrink from too much attention, we want to be admired, fawned over, and told how beautiful we are. We can't help it. We are Sanguine." Florence and I smiled at each other across the classroom.

Then Florence said, "Lest this example make us sound conceited or materialistic, Rose and I have both learned to turn our attention away from ourselves and make friends with the salesclerks. We realize that they need to know we appreciate all they do for us."

Since we understand personalities, we ask about their families and look at the pictures of their grandchildren. When our Sanguine needs are saturated, we sometimes turn the tables and suggest a new hairstyle that would look good on them. Often—when we have shown that we care about them, too—they will spill out their sad sorrows to us as we listen attentively. We try hard to remember their names, and we promise to pray for them. We know their emotional needs, and we want to meet them. Successful retail is not about exchanging material goods but about exchanging the "good" that every personality needs.

"Now we know the clerks in Chico's by name, and they know the two of us," I finished. "They don't rush to us just to sell us a new sweater but to receive from us an expected uplift of their spirits. Maybe life isn't so bad after all."

What Did We Learn This Time?

- People and profits are directly related.
- You might have to move your office employees around.
- Do put the Sanguine in charge of fun.
- Do put the Melancholy in charge of money.
- Give the Phlegmatic structure.
- Train the Choleric to be pleasant and patient.
- To sell the product, first know the personality.
- Remember there are people behind the personalities.
- Know that every personality needs a kind word.

16

Personalities in Ministry

Pastor Paul needed help.

When he'd first introduced himself to the group, he'd admitted that his congregation had found him—and his sermons—boring. Rose and I (Florence) knew that as a Phlegmatic leader, he probably had many more personality problems than that, including out-of-control Sanguines, miserable Melancholies, and pushy Cholerics. So we decided that this day would be good to encourage the group to open up and take what they've learned to help him and each other.

"Today Rose and I would love to see how well you've all been absorbing the material. We'd like to ask Pastor Paul to share some of his congregation's problems and have the rest of you offer any helpful insights you have from what we've covered so far. Pastor Paul, would that work for you?"

"Oh, yes!" he said. "You'd better believe it. I've been waiting for this session."

Rose had Carmen help her with passing out some materials. I called everyone's attention to the first handout—from my personality book *Getting Along with Almost Anybody*—and asked Pastor Paul to read.

Personalities in the Church

When our church needs a new pastor, we form some kind of committee and begin to have meetings at which we construct a profile of what we want in a pastor. The list usually starts by listing the weaknesses of the last dear man and making sure to look for the opposite traits in the new one. A better approach to selecting a new pastor would use an understanding of the personalities to recognize there isn't one perfect pastor. Rather, the pastor—and for that matter any business leader—will function best when someone is assisting them in the duties that don't come naturally to them.

When he was finished, I asked, "Pastor, does that sound like good advice to you?"

"*Yes*! Thank you, Florence! You *do* understand! It seems people in my parish want me to have the popularity of the Sanguine, the power of the Choleric, the perfection of the Melancholy, and the peace of the Phlegmatic. It makes me tired just thinking about it!" The group laughed.

"There's only one Person that perfect, Pastor Paul," I said. Everyone laughed again.

I recommended that they all read that book, since it includes a wide variety of stories from contributing authors that cover personalities in church, but that today we would focus on how best to place people in their ministry positions.

"Florence," said Pastor Paul, "I have so many problems in my office and I know most of them are personality issues. But—like I said—it wears me out to think about it. It's difficult enough to prepare a meaningful sermon each week . . . even though my congregation thinks I'm boring. Sometimes I just get so overwhelmed."

"Paul, you need some good, strong support!" said Holly Homes. She'd been keen on the pastor from the first class. "I've been thinking about how much I love the personalities and how I'd like to start using *Personality Plus* to teach this course myself, to my realtor friends, but maybe I can come to your church and do a fun seminar that would help your staff and congregation appreciate you more!"

Pastor Paul looked relieved and thanked Holly. "That would be nice. I see how well you handle people in real estate, and I bet you would be good at 'selling' personalities to people!"

I brought the class back to order and said, "Let's start. Pastor Paul, why don't you begin by sharing some of the specific troubles you have in your office? You don't have to tell us any names." He couldn't wait and began sharing his woes with the group.

"Well, to start, our youth minister is a highly qualified young man with a lot of ministerial degrees, but I think he's like me. Dull. No matter what we do, we can't seem to attract the youth to the group. Our last person was probably Sanguine—he always planned picnics, parties, and bus trips, and the kids loved him. But he ran off with one of the young schoolteachers and never even gave us any notice. All we got was an email about where to send his last paycheck. I figured a more serious and spiritual leader would be best for the teens."

"Ha! That's your biggest mistake right there!" blurted Howard.

"I agree," said Holly. "We're the Sanguines and we know! You probably *do* need a Sanguine, but one who is also spiritually mature. Kids need that high energy, but you're right, they need some depth and grounding as well. That's where your Sanguine could benefit from a team-teaching Melancholy. Or if you have a Melancholy in charge, get a Sanguine to bring the fun touch to the group activities."

"Yes," said Howard. "But if they're going to work together, they need to know how to appreciate each other."

"They need *this class*!" laughed Holly.

The pastor continued, "Okay, good. I like that. Team positions."

223

He went on. "I also have a Phlegmatic office manager. I see that now. She's humble and hard-working and is great at keeping things calm around the office. If an angry person calls or comes in with a list of demands, she's very poised and diplomatic, and she'll take care of the problem. But then she'll disappear the rest of the afternoon or call in sick the next day. She gets migraines and is completely drained by confrontation. What should I do?"

"Nothing," said Phlegmatic Hans Gutenberg.

"Nothing? What do you mean nothing?"

"Well, what I meant was there's nothing you can do about her getting drained. I think you should expect it and give her some time and space—that's what *Rose* always keeps saying—and let her recover. But you might also do something that I think I've learned from working with Darlene, my Choleric wife."

He looked at her with a smile, but Darlene looked a little worried.

"If things get really overwhelming, it's nice to know there is a Choleric somewhere who can step in for you once in a while. Not to do your job for you, just to help with the chaos or confrontation that may have built up. In our business, we can get some cranky customers and I'm usually okay with that. But every so often I just can't deal with them anymore. Darlene is a natural. It doesn't bother her at all to put people in their place."

Uh-oh. Everyone was silent at that last remark.

"I mean, she's great at handling the confrontation! Without getting drained. I really, *really* appreciate that in her now since we've taken this class," Hans said, backpedaling.

The group was laughing at poor Hans.

"Darlene, I love you, babe!" His face was red again.

Darlene took pity on him and gave him a warm smile in return. "I love you, too, honey."

Pastor Paul thanked Hans. "I do have a strong Choleric wedding coordinator who doesn't take any guff from anyone. She rejects the ridiculous music the couples want to have and has no problem with difficult people. After all, she regularly has to deal with the most dreaded horror of them all: the mother of the bride!" Everyone laughed. Pastor Paul was becoming humorous.

"Yes, I can ask her to be the go-to person for my office manager when things get too confrontational," he decided.

"What other problems do you have at work, Pastor?" asked Carmen. "I think I'll take all the ideas people are giving you and use them at my school office. They seem kind of universal, don't they?"

Everyone agreed.

"Well, the head of the women's ministry is a real handful. She's *very* spiritual, and even I'm not holy enough for her. She wants everyone to attend every meeting, fill out every form, read every spiritual classic, and do everything perfectly. At our last staff retreat she made everyone go on a full-day silent retreat. Very spiritual, but it nearly killed the Sanguines!"

Pastor Paul was very funny now! Howard and Holly were groaning and rolling their eyes at the very thought of a day of silence. The pastor seemed to enjoy the group's warm laughter. He wasn't used to that much response.

"She gets very upset and critical when people don't do things right. She even made a special appointment with me to tell me how I could be more spiritual," he said. "And she started with my sermons."

"Are you kidding me?" asked Fran Taylor. "Who does she think she is? The bishop?"

"No . . . GOD," said Pastor Paul.

And now the whole room was roaring. But the pastor had more on his mind than getting a good laugh from the class.

"She gave me this website where I could download the perfect sermon for any occasion. She'd already printed out six of them and put them in a three-ring binder marked "Pastor Paul Page— Sermons" and gave it to me. 'You can use the first one this Sunday,' she told me."

The pastor paused. His brow furrowed as if he were considering all he'd just shared. He heaved a heavy sigh and then looked up at the group.

"I did it. I did what she told me. I caved! I just didn't want to deal with her moods. Melancholy. That's how they control! We learned that before. Maybe that's why people fall asleep at my sermons; they stink! They come out of a can—like tuna fish," he added and chuckled.

The group was still laughing—*with* the pastor, not at him.

"Pastor Paul," said Dr. Hastings, "you are a gentle man with a good heart and—I'm sure we all agree—you have a natural humor that's very refreshing. I'll bet if you told some meaningful stories instead of using canned sermons, your flock"—he paused for effect—"would flock back to church!"

"I agree!" said Holly.

"Me, too," several voices chimed in.

The pastor looked relieved. "Okay. I'm going to do it. I'm going to 'can' those canned sermons!"

"Oh, *bro-o-o-other*!" groaned Howard, who laughed so hard his belly shook. "Give this guy a laugh or two and now he's doing stand-up!"

I asked the pastor to tell us what exactly he thought he might want to do in his church.

"First, I'll give a sermon about one of the best ways we can truly love one another: knowing the personalities. Then, I'll assign a team of all four personalities to schedule and have a seminar for everyone who's interested. We have a huge ministry fair coming up in a few months, and this will help everyone make sure they are signing up for areas that suit their natural strengths."

"Next, I'll have Holly come in, and I think together we can give a staff retreat that's fun and will help them understand their personalities."

Holly beamed.

"Then, I'm going to call my office manager and our wedding coordinator in and ask them if they'd like to work together in dealing with difficult people."

"Finally, I think I'll personally invite our women's ministry leader to sit next to me at our personality seminar. And, Holly, I'll delegate *her* to you! You can use your sales skills to help her see what a beautiful Melancholy she is!"

The rest of the day was filled with growing camaraderie and appreciation for one another. We enjoyed seeing these blossoming personalities and the fruits of everyone understanding the personalities. Rose wrapped up the session by giving everyone a copy of a helpful chart they could take to their own church communities.

It was time to remind our pleasant group that the next session would be our last class. I announced, "Next time is our end-of-session party. You are all going to graduate. Rose has a sign-up sheet in her hand where you can write down what you'd like to bring. And we're counting on you Melancholies to make our party perfect!"

"What if we don't know what we'll bring yet?" Howard asked.

Then Holly added, "Yeah, I don't know what I'll feel like making a week ahead."

Carmen turned to Howard, "Don't worry. I'll take care of yours."

Then Darlene announced, "I'll bring German potato salad done the way my mother made it—the right way."

"I'll peel the potatoes for my part," Hans offered.

"You don't need to do anything. I'll make a double portion. Relax. You can help me with the table settings." Then Darlene thought a second and added gently, "That is, if you want to do that for me." Hans nodded.

"I'll bring some little gifts," said Fran enthusiastically. "I've got some new samples."

"Can we eat them?" Howard laughed.

"I'll have to really think about this," Dr. Hastings murmured as Pastor Paul added, "I'll pray about it."

Working with and Placing People in Ministry

Popular Sanguine	Powerful Choleric
Prefers to be out in front Greeter, usher, song leader, hospitality committee personnel	Prefers to be out in front VBS director, Sunday school superintendent, fund-raising chairperson
• natural strength is friendliness • enjoys interacting with people • works well in a spontaneous and positive environment • prefers a fast pace with few restrictions • should be allowed freedom to be creative and spontaneous • seeks ministries that use his friendliness and relationship-building skills • should not work alone in ministry	• natural strength is getting the job completed • enjoys leading worthwhile projects • works well in getting new projects and ministries started • prefers to lead rather than to follow • should be allowed freedom to make decisions • seeks ministries that use her vision, leadership, and problem-solving skills • avoid maintenance-oriented ministries

Peaceful Phlegmatic	Perfect Melancholy
Prefers to be behind the scenes Ministry team member, nursery worker, nursing home volunteer	Prefers to be behind the scenes Secretary, treasurer, ministry schedule coordinator
• natural strength is cooperation and routine • likes being a loyal, supportive member of the team • works well following a good leader • prefers a steady and consistent pace • should spell out the parameters for her • seeks ministries that use patience and a warm and easygoing style • should avoid high-pressure ministries that require frequent change	• natural strength is compliance with the rules and guidelines • likes tasks that require information gathering and accurate detail • works well alone • prefers to know all the background and specific details before moving ahead • should spell out the parameters, allowing him to ask questions as needed • seeks ministries that use his organizational and accuracy skills • should avoid ministries that might draw lots of criticism from others

"Forget the sign-up," Holly called back as they headed for the door. "We'll just wing it and that will be fun!"

"I'll take charge and give you all a call during the week," Fran promised.

They went off happily, leaving Rose holding a blank sheet of paper.

What Did We Learn This Time

- Make sure that you train your staff or office in knowing the personalities.
- Learn where you may still be working in your weaknesses and make a change.
- Pair the Sanguines with Melancholies where necessary.
- Pair the Cholerics with Phlegmatics where necessary.
- Ask for group input once your staff knows the personalities.

The Farewell Party

Rose and I (Florence) had no idea what we should do in preparation for the graduation party—so we decided to do nothing and let the class handle it.

Fran Taylor had volunteered to take charge, and we had faith in what she would produce. We've all been to those company potlucks where no one cares, no one creates anything special, and the coleslaw is still in the clear plastic tray from the deli. But this group had learned to love one another. They really cared—surely they wouldn't come empty-handed.

When we arrived, Holly was already there. She had tacked up some crepe paper—red, white, and blue streamers—and was decorating the table with stand-up pictures of houses for sale.

"I chose really lovely homes and put the listing price on the back just in case." She had also already put one of her new three-fold brochures at each place. "So people will remember me," she said.

Next came Darlene with a huge bowl of potato salad, followed by Hans with a suitcase. She took one look at the bare table Holly had been decorating and said, "This will never do. We can't eat off plain Formica." She picked up Holly's pictures and brochures—as

Holly gasped—and asked Hans to help her set the table. He opened the suitcase and shook out a long green tablecloth.

"Green goes with everything. It's nature's prime color," she said.

Holly looked up at her patriotic streamers, which didn't go at all with green. We watched to see which one would win. Holly bit her lip, shook her head—and backed off, clearly deciding not to pick a fight with Darlene on the last day. She remembered her manners and quietly put her pictures back on the table.

Carmen and Howard came in together. She carried a large, lavishly decorated cake from the Cheesecake Factory and explained to us, "You can't have a party without a cake." We were all enthused.

Howard set a king-sized bucket of Kentucky Fried Chicken on top of some of Holly's brochures, but she was beyond reacting by then and didn't say a word.

"The Colonel makes the best chicken. You can't beat it," Howard said.

We could tell he was hungry. Fran Taylor asked why he didn't just bring food from his own restaurant, and he said, "That would be too easy. I have to set a good example for the others."

Fran had brought a little jewelry box for each person. "Earrings for the ladies and cuff links for the men." She gestured to get my attention. "Look, Florence. I wrapped them all up in silver paper with a bow on top, just like your book *Silver Boxes*." She was so proud of her thoughtfulness. I smiled and thanked her for her tribute.

She explained to those of us listening that the boxes were from the new line of her company jewelry, and she let us know there was an order form folded up in each box.

As Pastor Paul came in carrying a large urn of coffee, Holly ran to help him. He set it down and explained, "I knew we'd need a lot of coffee, so I made it at church and brought it over. I hope it's still hot."

Holly affirmed him with a smile. "It does seem hot."

He had a plastic bag looped over his arm. He opened it up and asked Holly to help him distribute his gifts. Next to Holly's pictures of homes, they placed an Upper Room daily devotional booklet and a brittle palm frond.

"These were left over from Easter," he whispered to Holly. "I couldn't bear to throw them away." They placed one on each china plate that Darlene and Hans had set down.

"I hate paper plates," Darlene was mumbling. "So I brought real ones. I hope everyone appreciates that these are our wedding china. Aren't they, Hans?"

"They sure are," he responded with a rueful smile meant to tease Darlene. Howard and Carmen both chuckled.

When Dr. Hastings entered, he carried two purple foil boxes. "I've brought the flowers," he announced. "Orchids for the ladies and a white carnation for the gents."

Hans seemed to be getting more into the party mood as he pinned an orchid on Darlene's ruffled dress. She thanked the doctor with a little hug.

As we all settled in with our meal of potato salad, chicken from the Colonel, and lukewarm coffee from church, we knew that cake would be coming to top off our weeks together. No one really cared what we ate. We were content just to be together.

Pastor Paul gave a blessing and—as we would all be going back to our respective lives and workplaces—asked the Lord to care for us "while we're apart one from another."

Rose put down her cup and began, "Do you remember the last night at summer camp? Everyone would gather around a roaring campfire, eat s'mores, sing songs, and cry because they had to leave their new best friends. That's how it feels on this last day of our 'Personality Plus at Work' class.

"Florence and I want to tell you all that we've enjoyed getting to know you and we hope you will consider bringing the personalities to *your* workplace," Rose said. "Now, suppose for a minute you're at your friend's party, and she's asked you to help serve a platter of yummy hors d'oeuvres to the room full of people, all unique, but half of them are the "same" because they're speaking only Spanish, and the others are speaking English.

"As you walk around the room, offering these delicacies, a beautiful dark-haired woman taps you on the shoulder and says, '*Una mas, por favor.*'"

"You'd probably think, *What? What did she say? What does she mean?* Do you know what to give her? Do you know how to help her? Do you understand what she needs? No! Because you don't speak her language.

"You wouldn't just walk away and grumble, 'Sorry, lady, I don't understand you so I'm going to ignore you.' If you care about serving her, you'll find someone to help you interpret what she's saying. And that's what the personalities are all about," Rose said. "It's not about putting generic labels on people but identifying what emotional language they speak, so you can either learn to speak it fluently yourself or get a translator to help you. That's us. We're your translators. If you use the quick tips and the handy charts we've given you, you'll be well on your way to becoming 'multilingual' when it comes to communicating with others in your workplace, your community, and your home. When we do this, we all improve our relationships, even though each personality will respond in his own unique way," she concluded.

Sanguines will be able to tone it down, get serious when necessary, and learn to listen to others, not gossip and cut short their fascinating stories.

Cholerics will learn to slow down and actually see and hear other people and give them credit for their ideas.

Melancholies will be able to speak words of authentic praise and encouragement, despite the imperfections that others have.

Phlegmatics will be able to speak up, speak out, and get to the bottom line instead of waiting for others to give the answers.

Rose then decided to tell a story she had never shared before. Her face lit up as she began, "Our last class is like a final reunion." Heads nodded. "And I have a personality story about recently attending my fortieth high school reunion. I walked in and looked around to see whom I recognized. Right away I saw my old boyfriend, Bob, who'd been my sweetheart in our senior year. "

Not only did I think he still looked handsome, but I knew immediately that he was a Melancholy-Phlegmatic. I recalled that Bob always played guitar, wrote songs, made homemade movies, and was in the school plays. He was definitely a creative Melancholy. He also never got really upset at anything and could get along with anyone, making his secondary personality an easygoing Phlegmatic. He didn't know the personalities, but I did and I knew I had him pegged.

"Wow, you look great after all these years, Rose!" he said. (I did, by the way.)

"Thanks, Bob. You do, too."

I was surprised that after forty years I was still excited to see him. As the night wore on, we reconnected in a warm, reminiscent way as we talked about the past. He mentioned several times that he was a "free thinker," and I just smiled knowingly. Creative Melancholies like to think outside the proverbial box. He told me that today he works as a professional voice artist on radio commercials and was doing some writing. More creativity. I smiled more and just listened attentively. Phlegmatics like that! Now that I recall, I listened to him go on with the details of the last forty years and I hardly talked about myself all night. I remember my mother telling me that men liked it when you listened to them. Funny how it had taken me most of my adult life to learn that lesson!

Bob was surprised when, eventually, I told him that I understood him exactly.

"You do?" he asked. "We haven't seen each other in decades." I knew that, like most Melancholies, he doubted anyone could really understand him.

"Yes, Bob, you *are* the sensitive, creative type!" And I began to list one by one all the Melancholy-Phlegmatic strengths from the study of the personalities. But I tried not to sound glib or know-it-all. Introverts don't like to be exposed. I've learned that beneath the exterior we all have sensitive hearts that no one can fully understand unless they are openly shared.

As I listed his many natural gifts, talents, and virtues, he listened and was utterly astounded. I'm sure in sensing my years-long affection for him he felt safe, and he opened up.

By understanding the personalities, we are all able to give words of encouragement to others that are sincere and authentic.

"Wow, you've just now touched me at my core. You crunched through the hard cherry candy and got right into that soft, chewy center of my Tootsie Roll pop." He was being funny but sincere at the same time. "*How did you do that?*"

"I laughed and thought, *Oh, Bob, if you only knew!*"

If only we *all* knew! By understanding the personalities, we are able to give words of encouragement to others that are sincere and authentic. We can get to know others, love them in the way they need to be loved, and help bring out their very best, at home or at work. Or even at a fortieth reunion.

The class liked Rose's story. Holly called out," Did you ever see Bob again?"

"Well, that's another whole story," Rose said.

She seemed to tone down as the women drew close. "Oh, tell us, please!" they bubbled out. Who can resist a love story?

"There's nothing definite to report, but we do see each other a couple of times a month. And we talk on the phone for hours every night. He lives five hundred miles away. We're rekindling the high school passion we once had," Rose reported, as if there was nothing more to say.

"What about that sparkly ring you're wearing?" Fran asked.

"Yes! You didn't have that when we first met," said Carmen. "We women notice those things."

"You girls notice everything!" Rose answered.

"Especially rings," they all agreed.

"Well, he told me he had to propose . . . because for the first time in his life he felt that someone finally 'got' him. He likes that I encourage his sometimes zany creativity instead of shaming him for it. I owe that to the personalities. In fact, I call him my 'Melancholy Baby.'"

Everyone laughed.

Pastor Paul—usually so shy and reluctant to contribute—stood up boldly and held his arms up as if he were giving a papal blessing and proclaimed, "I will perform the wedding ceremony!"

"Can we have it right here on this campus?" Carmen asked.

"Yes, we all know how to get here," Holly chimed in.

As Rose tried to wave them down from their newfound enthusiasm for a wedding, matronly Darlene burst out, "And I will be the flower girl."

The very thought of Darlene in a short, pink costume scattering rose petals made everyone laugh. Then Hans added, "I guess that makes me the ring bearer." More laughter, and then they all burst into singing "Here Comes the Bride." I could see we had lost control of the whole class.

Even Dr. Hastings jumped up, grabbed Holly, and swung her around as she called to Rose, "I'll sell you a house!"

Somehow real estate people never forget who they are and what they do. As I moved to the center of the class to regain control, everyone calmed down and settled back into their chairs. Howard asked, "Where is the wedding cake?" He always seemed to focus on the food.

"Let's get back to our program for this last day together," I said firmly. "Rose and I are going to give our own personality testimony and show you how our mothers didn't understand us. We hope this explanation will cause you to ask two things: how did your parents raise you, and how are you doing with your own children . . . or your co-workers? Rose, it's your turn first."

Rose seemed tired by all the shenanigans and thoughts of wedding details. But she pulled herself together and began.

No One Understood Her

"When I was small, I longed for my Melancholy-Phlegmatic mother's approval and acceptance and hoped for hugs and kisses that I never got. Deep down I knew Mom loved me, but it was hard for her to say it and hard for me never to hear it. Although I was rarely hugged or kissed, I did merit a few measured praises from her when I helped around the house."

By the time I was seven or eight, I was able to cook breakfast, fix school lunches, make beds, sort the laundry, and take care of the crying babies. When I did these things, Mom would show me occasional kindness with her tone of voice and a gentle Phlegmatic smile. But I don't recall her ever really praising me for my schoolwork ("That's fine," she'd say, "but you need to bring up those Bs to As"), or my entertaining antics ("Oh, Rosie, stop being so silly"), or any brilliant ideas that I shared. That's when I met her cold, blank stare and heard her matter-of-fact tone: "You don't know anything about that. You're too young. Let me tell you what I know . . ." and she'd launch into a long Melancholy lecture that would show me just how ignorant I was.

I also wanted to be beautiful like my mother and to have her tell me I was pretty. But she didn't. Mom was a striking redhead with delicate features, and she'd had modeling jobs when she was in her twenties. Like some mothers, I think she feared that if she were too generous in her compliments it might make me vain. So to save me from myself, she kept her mouth shut most of her life. And I kept waiting for a word—any word—of encouragement.

I was never able to be close to my mother, although over the years I tried. Then when I studied and taught the personalities with Florence, I began to understand not only my mother's Melancholy nature but also how her life history had impacted her. In the 1940s she'd been the first female chemist for Transworld Airlines (TWA) and had worked for Howard Hughes, a famous aviator, industrialist, film producer and director, philanthropist, and one of the wealthiest people in the world. Mom had college degrees and a brilliant mind and could have soared in a career, but she ended up stuck at home with all of us kids. I know she loved us all the best she could and I value all the many things she taught us, but until her dying day she stubbornly refused to let anyone inside her guarded heart. I began to see that as a Melancholy-Phlegmatic, she'd probably always felt that nobody ever really understood or appreciated her.

A few years before she died, she succumbed to dementia and hardly recognized or spoke to anyone when they came to visit. Although frustrating for our family, it was also a relief because Mom lost that hard, protective wall that she'd always maintained. I used to visit her in the nursing home and bring her favorite cookies. We'd sit in silence while she ate the treats and stared out into space. But one day, while I was sitting with her on her patio, she turned and looked straight at me. Her eyes were clear and bright, and with a sweet, almost surprised smile on her face, she said lovingly, "You're pretty!" And then, as quickly as the smile had come, it was gone, and she stared off again into the distance.

I was stunned! Not only had she spoken, but those were the words her Sanguine daughter had longed to hear from her for many years! And yet, when she finally said them, they didn't mean nearly as much as I thought they would. Immediately I realized two things: one, that those words had been there all the time; she just couldn't say them. And two, that as long as I stayed focused on what I couldn't get from her, I'd never be able to love her as *she* needed. I said quietly, "Thanks, Mom," and then I thanked God that somehow with the dementia came an unlocking of her heart.

"Mom died in 2003, but I treasure that moment on her patio where I was able to experience the natural kindness of the Phlegmatic and the sincerity of the Melancholy," Rose finished. "I *was* pretty, and she was finally free to tell me so. It was a powerful lesson in the personalities."

Holly clapped softly. "That was a beautiful story. I thought I was the only person who never got praise from her mother."

Getting the Words Out

After Rose had sat down, I said, "Let me tell you my story."

Rose and I have more in common than growing up in our respective fathers' businesses; our experiences with our mothers were also similar. My mother was a sweet, quiet Phlegmatic with the musical talent and depth of a Melancholy. Before marriage, she was a professional violin and cello player, conductor, and teacher. When she was thirty, I was born and the Great Depression had hit. My father was without a job and without income, and my mother was without pupils. In spite of bad times, my Sanguine-Choleric father stayed optimistic, borrowed money from a friend, and bought a small variety store. We moved into the building, and the store became our living room. There was one bedroom with double-decker beds, a tiny den with a piano and a couch, and an ugly kitchen.

My mother was trained to be a musician, but during those times there was no music in our family. As the only girl, I wanted nice things and a decent house. My mother would cry and wonder how she ended up like this. I felt sorry for her and my dad, and I would try to cheer her up. In a way, I became her mother. I did what I thought she should have done: I made curtains out of dishtowels and painted the blackened linoleum floor. I mothered my younger brothers, worked in the store, and studied between customers. My father—twenty years older than my mother—encouraged me in my love for the stage and took me to talent shows, where often I won the grand prize of two dollars. My mother never seemed to be proud of what I was doing and cautioned me not to get a "swelled head."

"Don't aim for anything too high, then you won't be disappointed," she'd say.

I kept aiming too high anyway and also led my brothers on to great achievements. When my wedding was chosen by *Life* magazine to be the event of the year, I thought my mother would be excited over my selection, but she dreaded all those strange people—those reporter types—coming into our store and the three pitiful rooms behind it. My mother said," I can't even go to the bathroom without getting my picture taken." For two weeks I rejoiced with every flash-bulb, while my mother did her best to keep out of sight. When the cameras walked in, my mother walked out. My Choleric mother-in-law bought all the copies of *Life* her local store had and passed them out to all her friends. She laid copies on her coffee table and began to look at me in a new light.

My mother never mentioned *Life* magazine again. From my wedding on, I would tell my mother of each of my advances and hope for her approval, but it didn't come. *Life* hadn't changed her life.

On the other hand, Fred's mother had no concept of what I did in real life. "Are you still doing your little talks, dearie?" she would ask. But she praised me for everything. "I'm so proud of you . . . in whatever it is you do."

When my daughter Lauren got married, we put on an extravaganza, including a forty-voice choir, singing "Is this the little girl

I carried" ("Sunrise, Sunset") from the Broadway musical *Fiddler on the Roof*. Fred's mother was exuberant and posed proudly for the photographers. My mother wilted before the cameras, and the pictures of her are all without the slightest smile and she appears angry. A few weeks later I called my mother, and in a sad voice she told me she was sorry she hadn't praised me more.

"I saw how you brightened up every time Fred's mother complimented you. You needed a mother like that, and I'm sorry. I've tried but I just can't get those words out of my mouth."

She never did get those words out of her mouth, but what a blessing it was to me that she was at least willing to say so. I hadn't realized how hurt I'd been until she let me know how sorry she was. She just *couldn't* do it.

Had I really understood that we are born with a personality and that my mother's Melancholy just wouldn't let her say the words I longed to hear, I could have accepted her nature much better and earlier than I did.

Isn't it amazing that Rose and I both lived in our father's business and both had mothers who just couldn't say, "You're pretty" or "I'm proud of you"?

"What people are you waiting to change in your family or your workplace? What co-worker, team member, or boss needs an encouraging word and you haven't given it?" I concluded. "My mother just couldn't get the words out of her mouth . . . how about you?"

Then I invited our students to share what they had learned. "Rose and I agree that you have been an intelligent and articulate group and one of the best audiences we've ever had. Before we close today, we'd love to hear your individual comments. Please tell us what you learned from this class and how you think it will help you in the workplace. Let's start with a Sanguine, because we know they are bursting to talk. Howard? Why don't you begin, and we'll go around the room."

Howard did something unusual for a Sanguine. "That's okay," he said. "Start with someone else. I can wait." Something was up, but we couldn't tell what it was.

"I'll start," said Holly. "First, I wanted to thank you and Rose. I have a mother like yours, too, who has yet to give me a compliment. This class has already helped me so much in how I see myself and others. I know it was about the workplace, but I'm seeing the four personalities everywhere I go!" She gestured with both hands to make her point. "I think the most important thing I learned was to be more sensitive to my mother and my Melancholy office assistant. I haven't really appreciated her, and she's been the one to keep all my title, escrow, and appraisal papers in order. I would never have closed as many deals as I have without her. And, Rose, I'm not going to give her a free lunch like you did with your people—I'm going to thank her and give her a nice Hallmark-type card instead of a silly one, a generous raise, and a day off!" She sat down, clearly quite pleased with herself.

Pastor Paul was next. "I want to thank you both, too. Florence, you are a brilliant speaker and you've inspired me to tell stories that touch the heart instead of taking the easy way out. There are some good thoughts in those prepackaged sermons, so I'm not going to unsubscribe just yet. But I am going to build my messages around a story I can tell easily. Like last Sunday. I told the story of how my father first took me trout fishing when I was ten years old and how patient he was in instructing me. I compared that to how God is also a patient, loving Father to us all. Everyone loved it, and one lady even said, 'You looked up today from your notes, and I saw you are really handsome.' I guess I had better keep looking up. So, thank you. *Thank you.*"

I told the pastor that Rose and I were privileged to be able to teach this class. We were just happy that he was happy! Then it was Fran Taylor's turn.

"I hate to admit this, but I never realized how pushy I am at work. I thought I was just getting everyone motivated. I never told you people this during our sessions, but most of the salesclerks in my company are Phlegmatics. They got hired because they could take orders and not make waves, but they don't sell much. I've already scheduled a personality workshop for them, and I'm going to take it regionally and hopefully nationally. Maybe internationally! That's how I think!" She laughed at herself, and the others laughed, too.

"And I am going to tell them all Rose's story of the Phlegmatic saleswoman at Chico's. They happen to be one of our competitors!" Fran concluded.

Hans didn't hesitate to raise his hand. "Darlene and I are next, but I'd like to go first. I have so much to say, but I'll keep it short and to the point." He looked at Rose and smiled.

"I have learned that my wife is the best thing that ever happened to me. And yes, she needs to slow down and be patient, and I need to speed up and get moving! There. That's it in a nutshell."

Darlene was laughing, and she leaned over and grabbed his arm. "Yes, everyone. Hans is right. There. I said it! We've already done what Fred and Florence did. We made a list of all our areas of responsibilities and divided them up. We're both much happier. And Rose, we both want to especially thank you for taking the time to share your own failings and misunderstandings with us. You have inspired me to be a beautiful Choleric woman, not a bossy one!"

Dr. Hastings was next, and everyone was waiting to hear what he had to say. He stood.

"Florence, this may sound melodramatic, but you have been the first person to ever really and truly understand me. In my whole life! I want to thank you from the bottom of my heart. And because of you I have made a major, life-changing decision."

He got a little choked up and looked straight at Florence.

"I'm leaving my practice."

Everyone gasped.

"Wait, it's not what you think. I've decided I have enough money for four more life spans—it's time for me to give more of my Melancholy gifts to those in need. I'm going to the mission field. I've signed up with Doctors Without Borders to serve victims of war and natural disaster. I leave for training next month, and I couldn't be happier. And when I see my new patients, the first thing I will do is assess their personality. And then I will know how to treat the whole person. And I have the knowledge of personalities to thank for that. I will be a much better doctor, and a much better person. I can't thank you enough." He sat down and let out a long, deep sigh of contentment.

The "pleasant group"—as the doctor had arrogantly labeled it in our first class—broke out in applause. When they settled down, he added, "And one more thing. I want to thank all of *you*. I came here thinking I had nothing to learn and that this group really had nothing to offer. I was wrong and I apologize."

Holly leapt out of her seat, went over and threw herself around the doctor's neck, giving him a big squeeze. "We all love you, Dr. Hastings!" Then she pulled back and said, "Oops! Is it okay if I hug you?" He laughed and hugged her back. "Yes, Holly. It's just fine!"

"What will your mother say when you tell her you quit?"

"I told her last night, and she asked, 'Will you make much money?' That's always been her greatest concern. I told her I'd be all right and she said, 'I hope so.' She's going to study what Doctors Without Borders is all about so she can brag to her friends."

There was a pause as everyone digested the doctor's news.

Howard finally spoke. "You're great, Doc. Carmen and I are the last two, and I'd like to go next. Okay?" He didn't wait for permission.

"Florence and Rose, I want to thank you, too. This class was fabulous. I already gave the personality test to my restaurant employees and they enjoyed it. We moved a few people around to

244

different positions and everyone seems to be happier now. I didn't have to fire anyone!"

He continued. "But the main thing I learned here is that I have always needed a Melancholy woman." He turned and looked at Carmen.

"Carmen, you have helped me with my diet, listened to my silly stories, and never put me down for being Sanguine. You're smart, beautiful, caring, and you fill in all the weak spots in my life. We've spent the last few months really getting to know each other and, well, all I want to do is learn how to love you and meet all your Melancholy needs. For the rest of my life. And yours." He paused and got down on one knee.

"Will you marry me?"

Carmen was trembling and blushing, but the glow on her face was unmistakable. Everyone grew excited.

"Say YES!" Holly yelled, jumping up and down.

"Shut up, Holly. Let her talk," said Darlene.

All eyes were on the beautiful, brown-eyed schoolteacher.

"Yes, Howard. I will marry you," Carmen said quietly.

The students all rose out of their seats and went over to hug the couple. Amidst the chaos we heard Darlene say, "Wait! Carmen, never got her turn to talk!" Suddenly, the room was quiet again.

"What has this class taught you, Carmen?" I asked.

Howard released Carmen from his embrace and stepped aside so everyone could listen.

Carmen smiled and said, "I have a new understanding of my students and I'm excited about being able to reach them more effectively. I plan to learn more about personalities, and I've already approached my principal about making it a continuing ed. course during the summer. And I think this will also make me a much better mother . . . when that day comes." She giggled.

Howard hugged her again tightly and whooped, "Yes-s-s-s!" For a long time we didn't think we could tear them apart.

Were You at Our Party?

While the others are enjoying the class celebration, realize that you should be at the party. You've done the work, you've read the book, and you are graduating, too. No longer are you crying over those strange people who just don't get it. No longer do you think, *Why can't they be like me*?

Because you know the answer: they were born that way and they probably won't ever change.

But you can give them this book. And while they may not find themselves on these pages, they might find you . . . and start treating *you* with understanding and respect—and perhaps even love.

Appendix A

Your Personality Profile

On the following pages you'll find our Personality Profile. Here's how to use it to discover your natural strengths and weaknesses:

1. In each of the rows of four words, place an X in front of the word that most often applies to you. Use the word definitions in appendix B for the most accurate results.

If you have trouble choosing between one or two words, check both—but no more than two words in each row.

Don't just check the reaction that you have learned, or what is expected of you in the workplace. Choose instead *your most natural and quick reaction in life*. Go back to your childhood; what word would you have chosen as a youngster? If you still aren't sure about which word best applies, ask a spouse or someone who really knows you. Ask, for example, "Do you think I'm more animated or adventurous?"

Remember that, at times, everyone can be animated, for example, but only one of the personalities is most *naturally* animated most of the time and in most circumstances.

2. Once you've finished, transfer all your Xs to the corresponding words on the Personality Scoring Sheet and add up your totals. For example, if you checked "animated" on the profile, check it on the scoring sheet. (Note: the words are in different order on the profile and scoring sheets.)

3. Once you've transferred your answers to the scoring sheet, added up the totals in each of the four columns, and added the totals from both the strengths and weaknesses sections, you'll know your dominate personality type by the highest total number. You'll also see your secondary strength. Remember that everyone has a blend of two natural types. It will be normal to have a few Xs scattered in all four categories, but two personalities should come out strongest.

Everyone is either part Choleric or part Phlegmatic but not both; these two are opposites.

Everyone is either part Sanguine or part Melancholy but not both; these two are opposites.

If you scored two opposite personalities (Choleric and Phlegmatic, or Sanguine and Melancholy), we suggest you ask your friends and family to help you with choosing your characteristics in the Personality Profile.

The two lowest scores will be those personalities that are not natural to you but which you *can* work to develop for a well-rounded personality.

If you've scored evenly between all four, there's a good chance you're Phlegmatic, because Phlegmatics are naturally most adaptable and can function well in every type. You might also be confused because you are unfamiliar with the terms (see the definitions in appendix B).

Another reason that two dominant types might not appear in your scores is that you have been masking (functioning in a type that is not natural for you) because of childhood pressures; expec-

248

tations from employers, spouses, and others; or a desire to be like someone you admire. The culture also pressures men to be Choleric. Your two natural types may be balanced, or one will dominate. The natural combinations are:

Sanguine and Choleric (double extrovert)

Choleric and Melancholy (extrovert/introvert)

Melancholy and Phlegmatic (double introvert)

Phlegmatic and Sanguine (introvert/extrovert)

Remember this is not an attempt to pigeonhole or slap a label on you or anyone. The test is to free you from any confusion about your natural, God-given gifts so that you can be your best in the workplace and enjoy what you do at the same time.

Personality Profile

Place an X in front of the word (or words) on each line that most often applies to you.

Strengths

1. X Adventurous	__Adaptable	__Animated	__Analytical
2. X Persistent	__Playful	__Persuasive	__Peaceful
3. __Submissive	__Self-sacrificing	__Sociable	X Strong-willed
4. __Considerate	__Controlled	X Competitive	__Convincing
5. __Refreshing	__Respectful	X Reserved	__Resourceful
6. __Satisfied	__Sensitive	X Self-reliant	__Spirited
7. X Planner	__Patient	__Positive	__Promoter
8. __Sure	__Spontaneous	X Scheduled	__Shy
9. __Orderly	__Obliging	X Outspoken	__Optimistic
10. __Friendly	__Faithful	__Funny	X Forceful
11. __Daring	__Delightful	__Diplomatic	X Detailed
12. __Cheerful	__Consistent	X Cultured	__Confident
13. X Idealistic	__Independent	__Inoffensive	__Inspiring
14. __Demonstrative	__Decisive	X Dry humor	X Deep
15. __Mediator	__Musical	X Mover	__Mixes easily
16. __Thoughtful	X Tenacious	__Talker	__Tolerant
17. __Listener	__Loyal	X Leader	__Lively
18. __Contented	__Chief	X Chart maker	__Cute
19. X Perfectionist	__Pleasant	__Productive	__Popular
20. __Bouncy	__Bold	X Behaved	__Balanced

Weaknesses

21. __Blank	__Bashful	__Brassy	X Bossy
22. __Undisciplined	__Unsympathetic	__Unenthusiastic	X Unforgiving
23. __Reticent	X Resentful	__Resistant	__Repetitious
24. X Fussy	__Fearful	__Forgetful	__Frank
25. X Impatient	X Insecure	__Indecisive	__Interrupts
26. __Unpopular	__Uninvolved	X Unpredictable	__Unaffectionate
27. X Headstrong	__Haphazard	__Hard to please	__Hesitant
28. __Plain	__Pessimistic	__Proud	X Permissive
29. X Angered easily	__Aimless	__Argumentative	X Alienated
30. __Naive	X Negative attitude	__Nervy	__Nonchalant
31. __Worrier	__Withdrawn	__Workaholic	X Wants credit
32. X Too sensitive	__Tactless	__Timid	__Too talkative
33. __Doubtful	__Disorganized	X Domineering	__Depressed
34. __Inconsistent	__Introvert	X Intolerant	__Indifferent
35. __Messy	X Moody	__Mumbles	__Manipulative
36. __Slow	__Stubborn	X Show-off	__Skeptical
37. __Loner	X Lords over others	__Lazy	__Loud
38. __Sluggish	__Suspicious	X Short-tempered	__Scatterbrained
39. X Revengeful	__Restless	__Reluctant	__Rash
40. __Compromising	X Critical	__Crafty	X Changeable

Personality Scoring Sheet

Strengths

Popular Sanguine	Powerful Choleric	Perfect Melancholy	Peaceful Phlegmatic
1. __Animated	X Adventurous	__Analytical	__Adaptable
2. __Playful	__Persuasive	X Persistent	__Peaceful
3. __Sociable	X Strong-willed	__Self-sacrificing	__Submissive
4. __Convincing	X Competitive	__Considerate	__Controlled
5. __Refreshing	__Resourceful	__Respectful	X Reserved
6. __Spirited	X Self-reliant	__Sensitive	__Satisfied
7. __Promoter	__Positive	X Planner	__Patient
8. __Spontaneous	__Sure	X Scheduled	__Shy
9. __Optimistic	X Outspoken	__Orderly	__Obliging
10. __Funny	X Forceful	__Faithful	__Friendly
11. __Delightful	__Daring	X Detailed	__Diplomatic
12. __Cheerful	__Confident	X Cultured	__Consistent
13. __Inspiring	__Independent	X Idealistic	__Inoffensive
14. __Demonstrative	__Decisive	X Deep	X Dry humor
15. __Mixes easily	X Mover	__Musical	__Mediator
16. __Talker	X Tenacious	__Thoughtful	__Tolerant
17. __Lively	X Leader	__Loyal	__Listener
18. __Cute	__Chief	X Chart maker	__Contented
19. __Popular	__Productive	X Perfectionist	__Pleasant
20. __Bouncy	__Bold	X Behaved	__Balanced

Total Strengths

0	9	10	2

Weaknesses

Popular Sanguine	Powerful Choleric	Perfect Melancholy	Peaceful Phlegmatic
21. __Brassy	X Bossy	__Bashful	__Blank
22. __Undisciplined	__Unsympathetic	X Unforgiving	__Unenthusiastic
23. __Repetitious	__Resistant	X Resentful	__Reticent
24. __Forgetful	__Frank	X Fussy	__Fearful
25. __Interrupts	X Impatient	X Insecure	__Indecisive
26. X Unpredictable	__Unaffectionate	__Unpopular	__Uninvolved
27. __Haphazard	X Headstrong	__Hard to please	__Hesitant
28. X Permissive	__Proud	__Pessimistic	__Plain
29. X Angered easily	__Argumentative	X Alienated	__Aimless
30. __Naive	__Nervy	X Negative attitude	__Nonchalant
31. X Wants credit	__Workaholic	__Withdrawn	__Worrier
32. __Too talkative	__Tactless	X Too sensitive	__Timid
33. __Disorganized	X Domineering	__Depressed	__Doubtful
34. __Inconsistent	X Intolerant	__Introvert	__Indifferent
35. __Messy	__Manipulative	X Moody	__Mumbles
36. X Show-off	__Stubborn	__Skeptical	__Slow
37. __Loud	X Lords over others	__Loner	__Lazy
38. __Scatterbrained	X Short-tempered	__Suspicious	__Sluggish
39. __Restless	__Rash	X Revengeful	__Reluctant
40. X Changeable	__Crafty	X Critical	__Compromising

Total Weaknesses

6	7	10	0

COMBINED TOTALS

6	16	20	2

Personality Profile Word Definitions

Strengths

1

Adventurous. Takes on new and daring enterprises with a determination to master them.

Adaptable. Easily fits in and is comfortable in any situation.

Animated. Full of life, lively use of hand, arm, and facial gestures.

Analytical. Likes to examine all the pieces for logical and proper relationships.

2

Persistent. Sees one project through to its completion before starting another.

Playful. Full of fun and good humor.

Persuasive. Convinces through logic and fact rather than charm or power.

Peaceful. Seems undisturbed and tranquil and retreats from any form of strife.

3

Submissive. Easily accepts another's point of view or desire with little need to assert his or her own opinion.

Self-sacrificing. Willingly gives up own personal needs for the sake of or to meet the needs of others.

Sociable. Sees being with others as an opportunity to be cute and entertaining rather than as a challenge or business opportunity.

Strong-willed. Determined to have his or her own way.

4

Considerate. Has regard for the needs and feelings of others.

Controlled. Has emotional feelings but rarely displays them.

Competitive. Turns every situation, happening, or game into a contest and always plays to win!

Convincing. Can win someone over to anything through the sheer charm of his or her personality.

5

Refreshing. Renews, stimulates, or makes others feel good.

Respectful. Treats others with deference, honor, and esteem.

Reserved. Self-restrained in expression of emotion or enthusiasm.

Resourceful. Is able to act quickly and effectively in virtually all situations.

6

Satisfied. Easily accepts any circumstance or situation.

Sensitive. Cares intensively about others and about what happens to them.

Self-reliant. Can fully rely on his or her own capabilities, judgment, and resources.

Spirited. Full of life and excitement.

7

Planner. Prefers to work out a detailed arrangement beforehand for the accomplishment of a project or goal, and prefers involvement with the planning stages and the finished product rather than with carrying out the task.

Patient. Unmoved by delay, and remains calm and tolerant.

Positive. Knows things will turn out right if he or she is in charge.

Promoter. Urges or compels others to go along, join, or invest through the charm of personality.

8

Sure. Confident, rarely hesitates or wavers.

Spontaneous. Prefers all of life to be impulsive, unpremeditated activity, not restricted by plans.

Scheduled. Makes and lives by a daily plan, and dislikes when plans are interrupted.

Shy. Quiet, doesn't easily initiate a conversation.

9

Orderly. Has a methodical, systematic arrangement of things.

Obliging. Accommodating, quick to do something another's way.

Outspoken. Speaks frankly and without reserve.

Optimistic. Sunny disposition, able to convince self and others that everything will turn out all right.

10

Friendly. Responds rather than initiates, and seldom starts a conversation.

Faithful. Consistently reliable, steadfast, loyal, and devoted, sometimes beyond reason.

Funny. Sparkling sense of humor that can make virtually any story into a hilarious event.

Forceful. A commanding personality against which others would hesitate to take a stand.

11

Daring. Willing to take risks; fearless, bold.

Delightful. Upbeat and fun to be with.

Diplomatic. Deals with people tactfully, sensitively, and patiently.

Detailed. Does everything in proper order with a clear memory of all the things that happen.

12

Cheerful. Usually in good spirits, promotes happiness in others.

Consistent. Stays emotionally on an even keel, responding as others might expect.

Cultured. Interests involve both intellectual and artistic pursuits such as theater, symphony, or ballet.

Confident. Self-assured and certain of own ability and success.

13

Idealistic. Visualizes things in their perfect form and has a need to measure up to that standard.

Independent. Self-sufficient, self-supporting, self-confident, and seems to have little need of help.

Inoffensive. Never says or causes anything unpleasant or objectionable.

Inspiring. Encourages others to work, join, or be involved, and makes the whole thing fun.

14

Demonstrative. Openly expresses emotion, especially affection, and doesn't hesitate to touch others while speaking to them.

Decisive. Quick and conclusive ability to make judgments.

Dry humor. Exhibits "dry wit," usually one-liners that can be sarcastic in nature.

Deep. Intense and often introspective with a distaste for surface conversation and pursuits.

15

Mediator. Consistently taking the role of reconciling differences to avoid conflict.

Musical. Participates in or has a deep appreciation for music, or is committed to music as an art form rather than for the fun of performing.

Mover. Is driven by a need to be productive, is a leader whom others follow, and finds it difficult to sit still.

Mixes easily. Loves a party and can't wait to meet everyone in the room; never meets a stranger.

16

Thoughtful. Considerate, remembers special occasions, and is quick to make a kind gesture.

Tenacious. Holds on firmly, stubbornly, and won't let go until the goal is accomplished.

Talker. Constantly talking, generally telling funny stories and entertaining everyone around; feels the need to fill the silence to make others comfortable.

Tolerant. Easily accepts the thoughts and ways of others without the need to disagree with or change them.

17

Listener. Always seems willing to hear what others have to say.

Loyal. Faithful to a person, ideal, or job, sometimes beyond reason.

Leader. A natural director who is driven to be in charge and often finds it difficult to believe that anyone else can do the job as well.

Lively. Full of life, vigorous, and energetic.

18

Contented. Easily satisfied with what he or she has, rarely envious.

Chief. Takes leadership and expects people to follow.

Chart maker. Organizes life, tasks, and problem solving by making lists, forms, or graphs.

Cute. Precious, adorable, center of attention.

19

Perfectionist. Places high standards on self and often on others, desiring that everything be in proper order at all times.

Pleasant. Easygoing, easy to be around, easy to talk with.

Productive. Must constantly be working or achieving; often finds it very difficult to rest.

Popular. Life of the party and therefore much desired as a party guest.

20

Bouncy. A bubbly, lively personality, full of energy.

Bold. Fearless, daring, forward, unafraid of risk.

Behaved. Consistently desires to conduct self within the realm of what seems proper.

Balanced. Stable, middle-of-the-road personality, not subject to sharp highs or lows.

Weaknesses

21

Blank. Shows little facial expression or emotion.

Bashful. Self-conscious, shrinks from getting attention.

Brassy. Showy, flashy, comes on strong, too loud.

Bossy. Commanding, domineering, sometimes overbearing in adult relationships.

22

Undisciplined. Lack of order permeates most every area of his or her life.

Unsympathetic. Finds it difficult to relate to the problems or hurts of others.

Unenthusiastic. Tends not to get excited about anything, often feeling it won't work anyway.

Unforgiving. Has difficulty forgiving or forgetting a hurt or injustice; apt to hold a grudge.

23

Reticent. Unwilling to get involved or struggles against involvement, especially when the situation is complex.

Resentful. Often holds ill feelings as a result of real or imagined offenses.

Resistant. Strives, works against, or hesitates to accept any other way but his or her own.

Repetitious. Retells stories and incidents to entertain without realizing he or she has already told the story several times before; constantly needs to say something.

24

Fussy. Insistent about petty matters or details; calls for great attention to trivial details.

Fearful. Often experiences feelings of deep concern, apprehension, or anxiety.

Forgetful. Lack of memory, which is usually tied to a lack of discipline and not bothering to record mentally things that aren't fun.

Frank. Straightforward, outspoken, doesn't mind saying exactly what he or she thinks.

25

Impatient. Finds it difficult to endure irritation or wait for others.

Insecure. Apprehensive or lacks confidence.

Indecisive. Finds it difficult to make any decision at all (not the personality that labors long over each decision to make the perfect one).

Interrupts. More of a talker than a listener; starts speaking without even realizing someone else is already speaking.

26

Unpopular. Intensity and demand for perfection can push others away.

Uninvolved. Has no desire to listen or become interested in clubs, groups, activities, or other people's lives.

Unpredictable. May be ecstatic one moment and down the next, or willing to help but then disappears, or promises to come but forgets to show up.

Unaffectionate. Finds it difficult to verbally or physically demonstrate tenderness.

27

Headstrong. Insists on having his or her own way.

Haphazard. Has no consistent way of doing things.

Hard to please. Standards are set so high that it is difficult to ever be satisfied.

Hesitant. Slow to get moving and hard to get involved.

28

Plain. A middle-of-the-road personality without highs or lows and showing little, if any, emotion.

Pessimistic. While hoping for the best, generally sees the down side of a situation first.

Proud. Has great self-esteem and sees self as always right and the best person for the job.

Permissive. In an effort to be liked, allows others (including children) to do as they please.

29

Angered easily. Has a childlike, flash-in-the-pan temper that expresses itself in tantrum style but is over and forgotten almost instantly.

Aimless. Not a goal setter, with little desire to be one.

Argumentative. Incites arguments, generally believing he or she is right no matter what the situation may be.

Alienated. Easily feels estranged from others, often because of insecurity or fear that others don't really enjoy his or her company.

30

Naive. Simple and childlike perspective, lacking sophistication or comprehension of what the deeper levels of life are really about.

Negative attitude. Attitude is seldom positive; often able to see only the down or dark side of each situation.

Nervy. Full of confidence, fortitude, and sheer guts, often in a negative sense.

Nonchalant. Easygoing, unconcerned, indifferent.

31

Worrier. Consistently feels uncertain, troubled, or anxious.

Withdrawn. Pulls back and needs a great deal of alone or isolation time.

Workaholic. An aggressive goal setter who must be constantly productive and feels very guilty when resting, is not driven by a need for perfection or completion but by a need for accomplishment and reward.

Wants credit. Thrives on the credit or approval of others. As an entertainer feeds on the applause, laughter, and/or acceptance of an audience.

32

Too sensitive. Overly introspective and easily offended when misunderstood.

Tactless. Sometimes expresses self in a somewhat offensive and inconsiderate way.

Timid. Shrinks from difficult situations.

Too talkative. An entertaining, compulsive talker who finds it difficult to listen.

33

Doubtful. Characterized by uncertainty and lack of confidence that things will ever work out.

Disorganized. Lack of ability to ever get life in order.

Domineering. Compulsively takes control of situations and/or people, usually telling others what to do.

Depressed. Feels down much of the time.

34

Inconsistent. Erratic, contradictory, with actions and emotions not based on logic.

Introvert. Thoughts and interests are directed inward; lives within self.

Intolerant. Appears unable to withstand or accept another's attitudes, point of view, or way of doing things.

Indifferent. Most things don't matter one way or the other.

35

Messy. Living in a state of disorder, unable to find things.

Moody. Doesn't get very high emotionally, but slips easily into low lows, often when feeling unappreciated.

Mumbles. Talks quietly under his or her breath when pushed; doesn't bother to speak clearly.

Manipulative. Influences or manages shrewdly or deviously for own advantage; *will* get own way somehow.

36

Slow. Often doesn't act or think quickly because it's too much of a bother.

Stubborn. Determined to exert own will, not easily persuaded, obstinate.

Show-off. Needs to be the center of attention; wants to be watched.

Skeptical. Disbelieving, questioning the motive behind the words.

37

Loner. Requires a lot of private time and tends to avoid other people.

Lords over others. Doesn't hesitate to let others know that he or she is right or is in control.

Lazy. Evaluates work or activity in terms of how much energy it will take.

Loud. Laugh or voice can be heard above others in the room.

38

Sluggish. Slow to get started; needs push to be motivated.

Suspicious. Tends to suspect or distrust others or their ideas.

Short-tempered. Has a demanding, impatience-based anger and a short fuse. Anger is expressed when others are not moving fast enough or have not completed what they have been asked to do.

Scatterbrained. Lacks the power of concentration or attention, flighty.

39

Revengeful. Knowingly or otherwise holds a grudge and punishes the offender, often by subtly withholding friendship or affection.

Restless. Likes constant new activity because it isn't fun to do the same things all the time.

Reluctant. Unwilling to get involved or struggles against it.

Rash. May act hastily, without thinking things through, generally because of impatience.

40

Compromising. Will often relax his or her position, even when right, to avoid conflict.

Critical. Constantly evaluating and making judgments, frequently thinking or expressing negative reactions.

Crafty. Shrewd; can always find a way to get to the desired end.

Changeable. A childlike, short attention span; needs a lot of change and variety to keep from getting bored.

Notes

1. Dick Thompson, Frederic Golden, and Michael D. Lemonick, "The Race Is Over," *Time*, July 3, 2000.

2. The *Summa Theologica* (or the *Summa Theologiæ* or simply the *Summa*, Latin: "summary of theology," written 1265–74) is the most famous work of Thomas Aquinas (ca. 1225–74).

3. Caitlin Flanagan, "Is There Hope for the American Marriage?" *Time*, July 2, 2009, www.time.com/time/printout/0,8816,1908243,00.html.

Florence Littauer, an internationally known speaker and author, has written more than forty books. Her book *Personality Plus* has sold more than two million copies in thirty languages. Other books include the bestselling *Silver Boxes, Personality Plus for Parents, Personality Plus for Couples, Personality Puzzle, Making the Blue Plate Special, How to Get Along with Difficult People, Your Personality Tree,* and *Daily Marriage Builders for Couples.*

Rose Sweet is a popular speaker and author of *Healing the Heartbreak of Divorce, Healing the Divorced Heart* (a devotional), *How to Be First in a Second Marriage,* and *Dear God Send Me a Soul Mate.* She has contributed to many other books, including most recently *Freedom: Twelve Lives Transformed by Theology of the Body.* Rose is co-producer of the landmark DVD series *The Catholic Divorce Survival Guide.* Rose incorporates the personalities into all her work.

Florence Littauer's Classic Bestselling Book

MORE THAN 1 MILLION SOLD

How to Understand
OTHERS
by Understanding
YOURSELF

personality
PLUS

FLORENCE
LITTAUER

Appreciate your one-of-a-kind, God-given personality. Improve upon your strengths. Correct your weaknesses. *Personality Plus* is the tool you need to change your life, and the lives of those you care about, for the better.

Revell
a division of Baker Publishing Group
www.RevellBooks.com

Available wherever books are sold.